Failed to Negotiate the Deal

TONY

HOPE

CAN FIND SOME

VALVE IN THIS

BOOK — ENJOY!

PAUL

603-661-0011

Failed to Negotiate the Deal

THE ART OF STREET-SMART DEALMAKING

Paul Hamblett

Columbus, Ohio

FAILED TO NEGOTIATE THE DEAL

The Art of Street-Smart Dealmaking

Published by Gatekeeper Press

2167 Stringtown Rd, Suite 109

Columbus, OH 43123-2989

w w w . G a t e k e e p e r P r e s s . c o m

Library of Congress Control Number: 2022932286

ISBN (paperback): 9781662925504

eISBN: 9781662925511

About the Title

I grew up in Derry, New Hampshire which was a small town near the southern border to Massachusetts. We were just a short ride north from Boston where we inadvertently acquired a unique accent absent of R's, and our real-life education came from the streets.

Derry was a very tough, blue-collar town with plenty of rough, hard drinkers and partiers. As boys, we called ourselves Dubba's from Derry or simply a bunch of dipshits. One thing in common though, was we were all a bunch of hell raisers. Things only got worse as we started turning 16 and getting our driver's license. Most of the families were financially disadvantaged, so seeing parents driving around in new cars was a rarity. For us boys, having a decent used car was difficult and what we drove was borderline undrivable, with dents, faulty brakes, exhaust, and transmissions. So, if we backed into something or hit another car it wasn't a big deal. In fact, the more beat up the car, the cooler it looked. We were horrible crazy drivers with no fear and it wasn't just us. The boys from the surrounding towns going down to Massachusetts were worse. I think the folks from Massachusetts are still the worst drivers in the country as we speak. Boys do grow up, but sometimes never change.

Because of our horrible driving skills, it was not uncommon to hear on the local radio station someone reporting car accidents. There was this one reporter who had this odd way of describing an accident. He would say something like this, "Two teenage boys, from wherever land, failed to negotiate a turn and hit a tree" or "A group of teenagers failed to negotiate a curve and rolled over." As you can imagine, the results of those negotiations did not end well. His accident reports were my first introduction to the word negotiate in a negative way.

One night I was with a friend of mine, Gary. Gary was an older, cooler guy who drove a late-model yellow Corvette. We were leaving a party after having had several beers. Both of us were tired and had a little glow going on. It was a very cold night in January and the back roads had 5-foot snow plow ridges. As we were driving around a corner, a little faster than we should've, we hit some black ice and spun around; we hit the plow ridge and flipped upside down into the road. We skidded about 20 feet upside down before finally coming to a stop. All of a sudden, everything was quiet and fortunately or unfortunately I didn't have my seatbelt on which was a once in a million-good thing. Trapped upside down in this tiny yellow Corvette, Gary asked me, "Buddy, are you all right?" As I answered, a small drop of blood dripped from the bridge of my nose, "I think I'm all right," which I was. I paused and thought to myself, I can hear it now from that radio reporter, two dipshits from Derry hit black ice, failed to negotiate a curve, and flipped upside down. Both miraculously survived with little or no injuries.

The next day, I drove to the garage where they towed the car and I was amazed by the condition of the car and how we survived that crash. I then went out to the crash site and saw the 20-foot yellow slide marks from the top of our roof on the black tar road. We were both very lucky that we weren't severely injured; however, my neck would never be the same. Two important lessons I learned from that vicious accident: the fear of loss, in this case, my life, is a great motivator, and failing to negotiate anything again would never be an option for me. That day I promised myself that I would never get in another vehicle with someone I didn't trust and, if I'm behind the wheel, I will slow down, be careful, watch out for the other guy, and be smart, not only academically but street-smart. Those basic rules would also apply to my future in business.

The phrase "failed to negotiate" has always stuck with me. It taught me the value of a successful negotiation, to proceed carefully and cautiously, and to never give up on the pursuit of common ground agreements. I call this the art of street-smart dealmaking because I've learned a lot by trial and error, exposure to all sorts of different folks, experiencing mistakes, and receiving valuable feedback from all the people I have negotiated and dealt with.

I hope you enjoy my journeys and stories in the chapters that follow. I want to share with you what I learned either by my own experience, classroom studies, or simply just being a street-smart guy of how to avoid failing to negotiate the deal.

Acknowledgements

Growing up, the traditional school system was not a good fit for me. Sitting in a classroom, listening to a teacher's lecture, reciting from a textbook, or giving their personal opinions was like a sleeping pill for me. Invariably, off I went into my own little world and would dream that I was the star high school quarterback, a young jet fighter pilot, a black belt in Karate, and yes, even a ladies' man. Unfortunately, I was none of those, but I could dream. In class, those dreams would quickly end, as the teacher would catch on and ask me, "Mr. Hamblett, where are you?" With chuckles from my student peers, I would come back to earth and continue my aloofness.

At home, it was a different story, I could lie in bed or on the couch, shut my eyes, and be anyone I wanted to be and I enjoyed it. I convinced myself that dreams can become reality and my pathway to knowledge was from people of all sorts. So, early on, I became a champion of people watching and a sponge for information. I was fascinated by people and would watch and listen to as many folks as I could. I had a thirst for their wisdom, experiences, their failures, and successes. I would look to see who was the smartest and most popular in the room and dream of repeating their prosperity. I figured out that the fastest way to be successful was to watch, study, and to listen to whom I wanted to model. It was intriguing to analyze people's energy, motivation, humor, charisma, and storytelling. For me, the world was my classroom and people were my teachers and I thank them all for a wonderful education.

I would like to thank Attorney Charles "Chuck" McIntyre, a brilliant litigator based in Washington D.C. Chuck was a client of mine, and fortunately for me, became a neighbor and friend. He took time out of his busy schedule, and with a fistful of red ink pens, helped shape a mishmash of content into something more coherent as a foundation for this book. His initial comments, that he found himself chuckling out loud and enjoying the read, gave me the inspiration I needed to finish this book. Thank you, Chuck.

Also, I would like to thank Kimberli Lewis, CEO of Global Business Therapy. Kim is an extraordinary coach and mentor and has more energy than anyone I have known. She is a close friend and I have enjoyed so many conversations with her about dealing with, influencing, and motivating people. We both wholeheartedly agree on the concept of people first, then the product or problem. Meaning, get to know and respect whom you're dealing with first, then go on to the business. She was also instrumental in convincing me that a storytelling approach is an effective way to communicate with people. Thank you, Kim.

Additionally, I want to thank the folks at Harvard Law school's Program on Negotiation. What an amazing program from one of the most prestigious law schools in the world. It was such an honor to attend their programs in such a setting of academic excellence and opulence. Their training is world class and the people and faculty I met were over the top. I am still in awe that I was accepted and completed one of their early Master Negotiation classes. Their concept of teaching a win, win approach as to negotiations, while expanding interests and options towards creating more value at the bargaining table, was truly enriching. Thank you.

Lastly, I want to thank all the people that supported me in this effort and the remarkable people I have met that helped shape this book.

Contents

INTRODUCTION

So, what's the big deal? The reality is that everything is a big deal. Whether you're dealing with your kids, boss, political rivals, or negotiating a big deal, trying to figure out what's important to them and what motivates them is the key to deal-making success. I quickly realized that to be successful in sales and negotiations, I had to figure out the age-old question of how to deal with all types of people. Trust me when I say that it is difficult to fully understand people, but not impossible. Everyone's DNA and fingerprints are quite different; so are their personalities. In a typical negotiation, I know what I want, and on the surface, I think I know what they want, but that's never enough information. It's the wise negotiator that knows there has to be more to the story than what's on the surface, so you have to dig deeper for more information. I do that with the three R'S, respect, rapport, and relationship. I ask questions and listen carefully to the answers. The objective is to find out what is really needed and wanted, while creating an environment where you can expand the value of the deal, without giving up your objectives. In other words, I want to help them win as well, without losing on my part.

In my early twenties, I studied Karate. We used to practice twice a week at night. It was a fairly large Karate school with two instructors. The head instructor was brutal. He preached intimidation, brute strength, and knockdown, drag-out fighting. The other instructor was an engineer by day. He taught us the mechanics of kicks, punches, and blocks. His approach to self-defense was quite different from the head instructor's. He taught us to watch and study our opponents. Watch their eyes, he would say, they give away their next move. He explained the concept of soft techniques. Using the power, aggression, and strength of our opponent, and using their inertia by gently sidestepping them before throwing them to the ground. His approach was not to destroy the opponent but simply win the match.

I applied his advice on the soft approach to my business. I learned from experience that dealing with people is a contact sport and in order to win, my opponent does not necessarily have to lose. If the head instructor from my Karate school was a negotiator, his approach would be statements like, "It's my way or the highway," "Take it or leave it." He would be very much a draw the line in the sand negotiator. He would use the bully approach and pound you with his fixed position. It would be very easy for his opponent to say, "I can't deal with you," or, "We agree to disagree" and walk away. I never wanted to walk away or terminate a negotiation that would be a failure. I simply wanted to find ways to keep the parties talking, with respect I must add.

So, the objective of this book is to try to convey to you that there is a soft approach to sales, negotiations, and mediation that works. I will do my best to illustrate through my experience and training an approach that more often than not works for me. I will do this with stories, anecdotes, and simple concepts that are not scientific or a boring study of human behavior. Just simple street-smart techniques from a guy who did a lot of deals and took a lot of punches.

I will end each chapter or story with the phrase "so what's the point," where I will summarize the main message and focus on a takeaway. I hope you will read and enjoy this book and at the very least get a couple of gold nuggets and chuckles. Enjoy the ride... Paul

RAPPARS POINT

In my thirties, I thought it was a good idea to take flying lessons as a new hobby as a diversion from the hard work and stress that was going on in my life. I started taking lessons at a small grass airstrip in Hampton NH, which was known for its small fleet of Piper Cubs. In my mind, a Piper cub was simply a go-cart in the sky. It was a two-seater, seating back and front, and the controls were stick and rudder. My instructor was barely 18 years old and when we would fly, he would get bored and take over the controls and chase Seagulls, just to show me how agile and responsive the plane was. But as reckless as I thought my instructor was in the air, he was dead serious about safety and had a thorough knowledge of the airplane and its moving parts. Before each flight, he completed a detailed walk around checking out the entire exterior of the plane with serious detail, which he called his pre-flight inspection. Once in the plane, he taught me another preflight inspection process, which had an acronym called CIGARS. CIGARS was a word that would prepare me for a safe departure and flight. Essentially, CIGARS was a memorized checklist before take-off to check the Controls, Instruments, Gasoline, Attitude, Run-up, and Safety. In the end, I was not cut out to be an aviator, but I learned a lot, especially the idea of the pre-check and an acronym to give me a memory system or plan before I started anything.

In negotiation and deal-making, I related it in some way to flying. I needed to take off, maneuver, and eventually land. In Negotiations, I needed to start the negotiation, deal with it, and eventually close the deal. Piece of cake. So, I developed a pre-negotiation checklist that I called RAPPARS POINT which would give me a basic checklist of items that would help me jump into a negotiation cold turkey. The following is what I thought were the essential concepts of an overview that would prepare me for the fun.

R	Respect
A	Assumptions
P	Parties
P	Players
A	Authority
R	Relationship
S	Stakeholders
P	Position
O	Options
I	Interests
N	Needs
T	Talk.

So, what does this all mean? Let's find out.

Respect. This is one of the most important words out there and best of all it's free. It's been said that you have to earn respect, but for me, it's always been beneficial to give respect upfront, with no conditions. Everybody wants, needs, and deserves respect, so my attitude is giving it to them upfront and giving them the dignity they want, while maintaining a healthy rapport throughout the negotiation. Some of my peers have questioned my good oh boy approach, but I honestly don't see the logic or productivity of not giving respect to my counterpart early on. I understand they may not deserve it, but in the end, I want to put a deal together and I prefer not to judge, but simply end with a positive result. So always respect one another right from the get go.

Assumptions. This is kind of a follow-up to respect. I never go into a negotiation with a fixed thought of my counterpart or what their intentions are. I plan ahead and do my pre-checklist, but walk in with an open mind. You give respect, flush out any assumptions, and maintain a clear head. This sometimes can be infectious, as your counterpart can also learn from your actions and follow suit. You want to create an environment where you all have free-thinking, no ax to grind, and create the ground rules for productive dialog.

Parties. Parties and players can be confusing, however very important to distinguish. Parties in this context is who I am dealing with. Call them the front person, lead person, or the bad cop in some cases. Whatever the label, your initial counterpart. These are the type of folks that are somewhat disguised as a true negotiating partner; however, their real role is intelligence gathering and a temperature check to jump-start a negotiation for other folks. The important part is to figure out if this person is capable or authorized to make any decisions, most likely not.

Players. Now, this is the person that can be the back-room person, or the person at the table who is quiet, yet listening intently. This is the person who really makes the decision, yet likes to take the back-seat approach to the process. Once you figure this out, it will help guide you through a more inclusive and productive dialogue. Let's assume you're a real estate agent and you are dealing with the husband. He's asking all the questions, beating his chest, and making it seem like he is running the show. Not so quick, his wife is listening, analyzing, and processing everything you say. Not only words but your approach, sincerity, trustworthiness, and authenticity. The bottom line is that she is one that makes the decisions and if you ignore her, come off as condescending, or brush her off as a sideshow, you will get absolutely nowhere. So, when you're selling, negotiating, or settling a dispute, figure out the party you're dealing with and the player that makes the decision as soon as you can. For when you figure that out, you can talk at the party you're dealing with but your message is really aimed at the player that can make the decision.

Authority. Sometimes you will have to deal with individuals, teams, groups, committees, or some kind of backroom big wheel. Trying to figure out who you're dealing with and who makes the decisions can be confusing.

I remember I was negotiating a large commercial real estate property for an international construction company that I worked for. We were the sellers and the buyers were a Fairly large development company that I was not totally familiar with. I was the Vice President of our New England office and was authorized to make a deal. The buyers asked me to meet them at their office to discuss a potential transaction. When I arrived, all by myself, they placed me in this huge conference room and then, what I thought was a small army, marched in a group of about 10 people. I said to myself, you gotta be kidding, I thought there were only going to be a couple of people here. So, the original person I was dealing with, who had all the pricing information as well as all of the documentation for the property, opened up the meeting with an introduction of all the attendees. Within seconds, I am getting peppered with questions about details, pricing, and terms from every which direction. I felt like a goalie for a dart team. I answered and deflected all of their shots and made sure I would do my best to answer all of their questions without getting trapped into a position. After a while playing a respectable defense, I decided it was the right time to go on the offense to determine who was the deal-maker. I had trained myself about the concept of Parties and Players, so now I became the person with the question. With key questions to some of the folks about their involvement with the project, it was easy to determine the accountant, project manager, land engineers, and attorneys. For the remaining folks, that I was unsure of, I simply asked straight out each individual, what is their role in the project. Finally, I figured out that the quiet person on the side of the table was the actual buyer... Volar! With proper eye contact and a confident smile, I zeroed in on the buyer/decision-maker and looked at him point-blank and said to him, you have all the information, what are your thoughts, are we able to do business. He smiled at me, and I think he was genuinely impressed by how I took all of his staff's shots and questions and said yes, we can do business. We tweaked the price and dealt with terms and eventually closed on the deal.

So, figuring out who the dealmaker is can be a challenge but not impossible. Crafting a relaxed, freewheeling atmosphere and asking key questions as to one's involvement typically uncovers the dealmaker. These are necessary steps to effectively and accurately consummate a deal.

Relationship. Respect and maintaining a long-term relationship are in my mind constantly. I have had friends that basically said if you're only going to do one deal with this person, then go for the jugular and pound these people and get the best deal at any cost. I guess if you're only going to this one deal and then move to a remote island, maybe you can justify this tactic. But for those of us that are in it for the long run, having a good relationship with someone is like having a good reputation. I think those two RR'S go hand and hand and I personally made them a standard in my career. Having a good relationship, or building a sincere rapport with someone is infectious; it can be reciprocal and rewarding. However, the take no prisoner approach, the I win you lose strategy, and box them in a corner scenario, may be a short-term win, but a long-time loser. Words travel fast, especially bad words and pissed off people. You may never deal again with this person you just took advantage of, but guess what, they have friends, family members, and business colleagues that will hear the whole story, so forget about any relationship, you just lost your reputation. I have dealt with many deals and disputes with people I did not know, but with their research, they have often found someone that knew me and said, oh yeah, he's a good guy you can trust him to work with... priceless. Do your absolute best to maintain great relationships with as many people as you can, it's the right thing to do, less stressful, and can make things move much easier.

Stakeholders. These are the folks that sit on the sideline that are part of the deal in some way, shape, or form. They may or may not be at the negotiation table, but they still have input and influence and it is very important to identify them. These folks are your silent allies and can be critical in influencing the direction of a negotiation. In the simplest example, you're a real estate agent and you're dealing with the husband, but the wife actually makes the decisions; however, the children, AKA the stakeholders, can have a significant say on what they like and will make them happy.

Stakeholders or influencers are particularly important when a deal is not going well. What if you had a software program that you're trying to sell to a company that is quite pricey, yet highly advanced and in your mind could be very beneficial to this potential client. The buyer is hung up on price and really is afraid of change and you're getting nowhere. You did your needs analysis and prove to the buyer that this software will increase sales and productivity, but the buyer is stubborn and resists. Rather than call it quits and chalk up a no, it's time to head for the hills and find some stakeholders. What would happen if you somehow bumped into the CFO of the company and gave them your elevator speech and explained how this software would generate additional revenue, cut costs, and would win the cost versus benefits analysis. Even better, what if you miraculously ran into a couple of their sales folks at a bar or restaurant and were able to give them a pitch on how they would get more inquiries, leads, and clients with this software. Now you may have your own private sales force working on the buyer. There are always an ample group of stakeholders and influences out there. Sometimes you need them, sometimes you don't. But always identify them and keep them in your back pocket if things are not going well.

Position. How many times have I heard that it's my way or the highway, the line in the sand, this is my final offer, I am firm on price, this is non-negotiable or my least favorite, we agree to disagree. Taking a firm position on price, terms, products, and a particular stance is your own personal trap to failed negotiations or dispute resolutions, pure and simple. The wise negotiator will never put up a roadblock or firewalls that could cut short or end a conversation. Negotiations are a work in progress and should always be fluent and no one should get stuck in a fixed position. Egos and personalities play a huge role in keeping a conversation going, but it's the master that will keep everybody talking and getting concessions. It's easy to get frustrated and throw in the towel and say, I am done. But the smarter ones at the table will not allow an endpoint without an agreement and will also help his counterpart stay free flowing and brush off their fixed positions as simple hard-liner tactics. When someone is fixed on a particular position, not only does it put an agreement in jeopardy, but it does not allow the parties to participate in a creative environment on how to brainstorm everyone's goals and desires. If you know what you want, that's OK, just find the right route to take and don't be afraid of recalculating... just don't stop.

Options. So, what are the options? Not sure, let's try and figure it out. There are always options, alternatives, and endless possibilities if you and your counterpart are open to creativity. We have talked about respect and having a good relationship with the parties of the negotiation or dispute, which lays the groundwork for brainstorming for what can be added or deleted from whatever you're trying to achieve. In the real estate business, I referred to potential offers with the concept of price and terms.

We were working on purchasing a commercial property and the asking price was $1,000,000. We clearly wanted the property, but we had to figure out what motivated the seller. We already had done due diligence on the property and had a good idea of what the highest and best use was. Our first offer, or so we say, option number one was for $850,000. Cash deal and closing in 60 days. No way they said. Our second option was for full price, with some owner financing and 120 days to get the approvals needed to do what we wanted. Not interested, they said. So, two things we learned is the price is a concern and they did not want to do owner financing. Our third offer/option was that we would offer $925,000 for the property subject to having 120 days to get the approvals for what we wanted. They said you have a deal! They received the price they wanted and we received the terms we wanted.

I remember once I was dealing with a company that provided software for a complete management system for our office. I have to admit that I am not the sharpest tool in the shed; when it comes to technology, however, I am bright enough to know how to ask questions and seek alternatives. In their initial presentation, they explained all the bells and whistles of their programs and the cost and monthly fees. I said no way do I need all of your features and the cost is way too high. Now I did not want to create a room full of tension, so I asked the lead sales guy if he liked steak. He said yes, I sure do. I asked him if he heard of Ruth Chris steakhouse. He answered sure. Ok, let's pretend your program is the Ruth Chris of software, which if you are familiar with them serves up a top-notch prime steak; however, everything else is A la carte. So now let's brainstorm. I want your base program, but let us focus on my exact needs that would fit into my budget and dismiss all the features that I am not interested in. The key to developing additional options is to create a cordial environment where folks are free to discuss additional choices, alternatives, and possibilities.

Interests. Interest and options are somewhat similar but interests tend to be more personal in nature. But they do share an important characteristic. They both have to be developed in a cordial environment that would encourage greater choice and creativity. In negotiation, it is vital to find one's needs, wants, and urgencies, and getting that correct information can be a challenge. I have always said, I can deal with the known, but I can't deal with the unknown. Meaning if I do not know my counterpart's true feelings and needs, the negotiation or dispute will go nowhere. Asking questions, finding likes and dislikes, talking about things unnrelated to the negotiation, and simply having laughs or diversions can open up one's mind to find the truth... what they need, want, and urgencies. I remember the old negotiation 101 days when they talked about splitting the pie. To be fair you get half and I get half, simply no argument. I put a little twist on that concept with my wife. We both love pizza and our favorite place is Santarpio's Pizza in East Boston. The place is an old, Italian no-nonsense pizza parlor. This is a place where if you asked for a Hawaiian pizza with pineapple, they would throw you out.

Also, they don't have a small, medium, or large pizza, just one 14-inch size and that's it. We normally get their salad; it's an easy choice because they only offer one choice. It's big enough to split and I let my wife take what she wants and I eat the rest. That negotiation was simple as I like the salad, but the amount was not important to me. Fortunately, we both like sausage and garlic pizza. The initial tension for me was that the 50/50 concept was not for me. With 8 slices total, 4 was not enough for me and I wanted 5 slices. I quickly found out that my wife is a crust person. That is so awesome because I am not; I find the crust just to be handles to eat my pizza and pile them up off to the side. She asked me if she could eat my crusts and I said sure and by the time she had her third piece and my crust, she was full and I had my five slices. Had I not paid attention, I would not have known that she was interested in the crust.

Pretend you're negotiating a labor dispute and you represent the employer. Your counterpart represents labor and is threatening a strike if they do not get their way. But what is their way, or better put, what are they really interested in? Their negotiator does a shotgun approach to what they want, which would include higher wages, better health care, deductibles, pensions, sick leave, and anything else they can throw in. Your job is to figure out what the top interests are and deal with them. You approach your counterpart with the three R's, Respect, Relationship, and Rapport, you talk, listen, and do your best to have an open and honest conversation. In that environment you discuss wages and it seems that a modest annual increase would be fine. The pension issue is OK the way it is. What you finally zero in on is that the health care deductibles and the number of sick days are an issue, being a stressful job. You then say let's take a 48-hour break so I can do a little research on our issues. The first thing you do is call up your health care provider and explain to them the pickle you're in and see if they will renegotiate the premiums with a lower deductible. If you plead your case correctly, I am quite confident they will work with you. Regarding the sick days, they now get 5 and want more. The compromise would be to give them 8 in a calendar year, however only 5 could be carried over into the new year. They get extra sick days and you don't need to worry about the extra days being parlayed in the years to come.

You set up another meeting and offer the following changes to their contract: Wages will increase for the next three years at a 3% increase, deductibles will be cut from $2,000 to $500, and sick days will increase to 8 days. Hopefully, you will have a done deal. The better you're able to get to know someone, the better you are able to discover the real needs, wants, and additional interests.

Needs. I would say the fundamental tension in a negotiation or dispute is one's needs. I tend to talk about needs, wants, and urgencies, but the first challenge is determining what you and your counterpart really need. Sure, we will try to tweak additional options into the deal and yes, we will figure out mutual interest, but needs are our ground zero. Believe it or not, sometimes people don't know exactly what they need or want. They think they do, but after many conversations, you can discover that they are really open and flexible to what they need. I remember early on in my real estate career, the old-timers would say that "Buyers are Liars". I thought that statement was cruel and quite frankly obnoxious, and I was of the opinion that the customer was always right. After a while, I figured out that the old-timers were right, sometimes buyers would set down a list of needs in a home and you end up selling something that was the complete opposite. I remember early on in my career, I was working with a couple that when we had our initial meeting we sat down and they gave me their exact needs for what they wanted. They wanted a colonial home, attached two-car garage, 3,000 square feet, and no more than a half-acre of land. I then went out to show them five homes that matched those descriptions and got five no's. What's up with that, I said to myself. The good news for me was that I was smart enough to review with them why they did not like each home and was better prepared to hone in what I thought they needed. Armed with the new information, I put myself in their shoes and knowing the marketplace, what would I choose for them. My choice for them was a 2,800 square foot cape style home, with an attached three-car garage and a wonderful two-acre lot. Not even close to what they originally described but they bought it and I learned a very important lesson that needs can be a moving target. The successful negotiator will hear and listen to one's needs but will go a few steps ahead and find if those needs are flexible and seek alternatives.

Talk. For me, this one was easy. So easy that I found out quickly that I talked too much. In today's world of email, texting, and social media, we find it easy to let our fingers do the talking and if we get really emotional, we throw in a few emojis. I believe there is a time and place for this type of communication, but in business and negotiations, you have to be careful. It's hard to interpret one's true intention with a simple text. It's also difficult to measure one's emotions and sincerity with an email. I always said when the deal gets tough, I get talking.

I remember one of my agents was working with a younger couple to sell their existing home and find them a new waterfront home. The couple were very bright technology people and did not have any kids and were focused on their careers. So, my agent listed their home for $500,000 and their new price range was $1,000,000, a sizable transaction. The house gets listed and the agent is doing everything he should do to market their home. In a short time, he received several offers on the home and a barrage of questions for the sellers. He emailed the offers and questions to the seller and by their responses, they seemed annoyed with his handling of their property. The offers are too low and the questions are stupid, they wrote back. In reality, the questions and offers are a healthy natural process and necessary to get to an actual offer that would be acceptable, but the point was not getting across through his emails. After a few days, my agent comes storming into my office fit to be tied and says he wants to fire his clients and wants to know the process. I said to calm down, and tell what the tipping point was. He said he received an email from them late last night and it was downright disrespectful and questioned his abilities to successfully sell their home. I asked him what time they sent the email. He said it was 11:30 at night which I found to be rude and the email was filled with exclamation points. The bottom line is, I have had it with these people. I asked him when was the last time you have talked to these people. He said we have been in constant communication via text and email. I asked again, when is the last time you have talked to these people. It's been a few weeks, but you have to understand, these are technology people. Here's the deal, I said, I can visualize these folks sitting around in the living room and drinking a few glasses of wine and saying let's torture our real estate agent, so they did. So, here is what I want you to do, pick up the phone and call them up and tell them you did not understand last night's email and if they could explain their concerns. I said I would not discuss the termination process until I hear back from you about what they have to say. I jokingly reminded him that sales and negotiations are contact sports. The next day he comes back to my office with a big smile. I asked how he made out. He said it was like night and day. They took my call and apologized for the late-night email and wanted to know if we all could meet for lunch. He said we all met and it was like a love fest... amazing. Their home was eventually sold and then he sold them another home for $1,100,000. So, the moral of the story is that it's easy to be tough and arrogant with your fingers, but for most people, tough to do with your lips. Don't ever be afraid of picking up the phone, or even better meeting them in person. The results will be quite different.

So, what's the point? The point is that having a checklist that can prepare you for a negotiation is a must, no different than a pilot getting ready to fly a plane. You can quickly develop a plan for how to structure a process, objectives, and figure out an approach to sell a product or solve a problem. The beauty of having a checklist is that if things are not going well in the conversation, you can revert back to RAPPARS POINT to review and alter your approach. Are you stuck in a position, working with the wrong person, not being respectful, or anything to steer you off course? The checklist is designed to eliminate the tension of what to do but guides you on how to do it.

PREPARE FOR TAKEOFF

Okay, now we have completed our preflight checklist and are ready for takeoff. Next, we need a flight plan towards our needs, goals, and visualize an optimum outcome. One of the first things to focus on is the concept of aiming high and reaching for the sky. In the negotiations training world, we call that **anchoring,** which means that whatever you're trying to achieve or accomplish, you would be wise to overstate your needs and wants. I know for a fact that whenever I negotiate, I am going to get beat up a bit. So, honestly, because I am fully aware of it, when it happens, I am not surprised and handle it easily. To be successful in deal-making, you need to be flexible, be a good listener, be ready to make corrections, and understand the importance of compromise. One of my favorite sayings is "even on the smoothest of waters and winds, my sailboat still requires a series of corrections to get to my destination." That is so true in deal-making. To exaggerate your situation is a logical concept, knowing that you may need to compromise. Maybe you won't need to cash in your added value if you present your case in a clear and methodical fashion that is substantiated with facts and figures, but you need to be prepared to do so.

Before we have wheels up, we need to imagine the perfect plan that will provide you with a flight plan of what you need and want to get to a final destination, meaning a positive outcome to a deal. Let's write down the key ingredients of a plan or as some folks call it, the wish list:

- Needs
- Wants
- Timing
- Pricing
- Priorities
- Terms and Conditions

Maybe it's not a money issue or tangible component that's part of the deal. It could have an emotional twist to the needs, such as;

- Show of respect
- An Apology
- Recognition
- Acceptance

Once you have established your list of needs and wants that represent your vision of a successful outcome, the next thing you need to do is to substantiate them with facts, figures, and data. Yes, this requires a lot of time and energy on your part, but the proper research will win you benefits with your counterpart if what you're asking for makes sense and sounds reasonable. There is so much information out there that is quite easy to use to substantiate your claims. Bear in mind that your counterpart may have to get approval to finalize the deal, or at the very least be accountable to other folks after the fact. By providing these facts and data, you may help them save face.

If you're buying a commercial property, find comparable sold sales to substantiate your offer.

If you are buying new software for your office, seek out competitors for features, pricing, and installation times.

If you're negotiating wages, find out what similar folks are making in other areas.

If you are negotiating potential litigation, make clear the cost of legal fees, the stress and emotions involved, and the horrible possibility of appearing in court.

Whatever you ask for in a negotiation, be prepared to defend it with a reason why it makes sense. Your counterpart may not agree with you, but they still may understand your requirements better.

You're at the table, you are prepared with what you need and want and have facts and figures to back them up, now what? It's all about figuring out what the other side's needs and wants are. It's also your job to try and control the tempo while maintaining an overall environment of respect. There is no doubt that someone is going to be the alpha dog, so if it's not you, by default it will be them. When I mention tempo, I also mean the time it takes from start to finish. The longer a negotiation drags on, the more complicated it can get. Your job is to build a rapport with your counterpart ASAP. The ideal environment would be that you are not adversaries to a deal, but partners in creating a deal. I suggest that you spend the same amount of time and energy you spend on figuring out your needs and wants to learn and understand what they need and want. If you listen and show an affinity for their situation, in most cases you will be returned the same favor. I liken my efforts to being similar to opposition research. I want to find who I am dealing with and try to get as much information on that person as I can. Once I've figured out that person, I may discover hidden details of how they operate and what motivates them. I simply want to get along and better understand my counterpart. I roll with the theory that maybe through open, honest dialogue, I can possibly make my deal better. Of equal importance, however, is seeing if I can help them achieve their goals as well. Why not? If I can find through our conversations that there are items of interest on or off the table that have little interest to me, then, by all means, let them have those. I am happy, they're happy, and we just expanded the value of the deal. It's not a crime or business embarrassment to help your counterpart get a better deal, more like a professional courtesy.

So, what's the point? The point is if you don't ask, you don't get. If you don't know what you want, you won't get it, it's that simple. In order to get your fair share, you need to prepare a list of needs and wants and rank them in the priority of importance. You also have to be able to justify your demands or requests with facts, figures, and criteria that will make sense to your counterpart. You need to create a respectful environment that allows for all parties to better understand each other's needs and maintain a relationship that will survive the deal. Never confront a person personally over what they want or need, simply focus on the individual pieces of their concerns. Keep your battles tiny and targeted.

PLAN B

Plan B is a huge negotiation game plan and without doubt one of your biggest assets or in the case of no Plan B, the biggest liability in your negotiation. In most formal negotiation training programs, such as Harvard Law School's Program on Negotiation, they teach the concept known as BATNA. Which is a simple acronym for **Best Alternative to a Negotiated Agreement**. Knowing your BATNA or simply put, Plan B upfront and completely thought out is vital to any successful negotiation. When you are going into a deal-making situation, we have already discussed knowing what you need and what you want. Needs being what you must have and wants to be like extras, that help sweeten your deal. Think of your Plan B as a backup plan if you can't achieve or negotiate your Plan A. Having a Plan B will provide you with a barometer for the strength of your bargaining power. If you have a strong Plan B, which should be your goal, then Plan A, your desired outcome must be a better deal than your Plan B or you simply say no and politely walk away. Having a strong Plan B will reward you with a strong position with your counterpart. With a strong Plan B, and by the way, don't be afraid to flaunt it to your counterpart, you're better able to control and affect the outcome to a more desirable agreement. What can be better than having a strong Plan B? In my world, I strive to develop plans C and D just for grins.

If everything is going well, you have created a detailed checklist of your needs and wants, which is your Plan A and you have a strong backup plan, Plan B. If Plan A is not achievable or reasonable, what else can you do to strengthen your position? Figure out their Plan B. Call me Curious George, but I want to go into the negotiation with all my plans in place, and even better, having figured out what my counterpart's Plan B is likely to be. I do that by talking. I buzz through my RAPPARS POINT checklist and the first thing I do is work to maintain a respectful relationship and rapport with my counterpart. I want to create a friendly environment in which my counterpart feels free to openly discuss their needs and wants. If I focus on their needs, rather than mine, by asking questions and listening to what they say, and keeping them talking, their Plan B may surface. Depending on the person, I could go off script and talk about sports, family, anything to figure out what type of person I am dealing with and try to find out any hot buttons on their part. But it's not just about trying to figure out their Plan B. Of equal importance is to try to open the door to additional interests and options that may appeal to them. I know this may sound crazy, but since I know what I need and want, I want to control the narrative and help them get what they want. By having an open dialogue, maybe there are items or services that I could provide to sweeten the deal at little or no cost to me which will help me get what I want.

What if you have a weak or even worse no Plan B? Not good, but you're going to have to deal with it. This is when you want to be a polite and professional poker player. You need to be quiet and confident and respectful toward your counterpart. It's a time that you need to create a conversation that's all about them and keep them talking. You want to slowly work on getting your needs and chip away at any of your wants. You want to avoid getting into any conflict, even at the cost of being a little submissive. You want to deflect any conversation regarding your long-term plans and strategies and keep the conversation about them. The strategy is to stay focused, positive, and promote a mutual long-term relationship.

In a more simplistic vision, we can say what are your alternatives or options? It's the negotiation masters that can develop more options, expand the pie, create more value, and orchestrate a harmonious tempo. But also, it's the players that need to focus on getting the job done, and working together is not a sign of weakness, but an air of confidence. Another important alternative not to lose sight of is to do nothing. I know from experience that no deal is better than a bad deal. I have worked with people that treated deal-making like a sport, they have to win at all costs. In their haste to get a deal, they skip over the concept of creativity and go for the jugular. There have been many times when I knew I could put a deal together; however, I just could not deal with my counterpart. There have been plenty of times when I have said let's take a break and get some coffee or fresh air. There may be a time when you need to confront your counterpart and simply say we are not on the same page and if we do not reset, this deal is going nowhere. I've always believed that honesty is the best policy. Walking away from a deal is risky business, but sometimes necessary. It's really important that when you bow out of a deal, you do it gracefully and respectfully. Leave the bargaining table without any fixed positions and simply walk away but leave the door cracked open. Avoid drawing lines in the sand, or giving ultimatums. Always leave with something open on the table, crumbs on the floor, or anything to keep your counterpart scratching their head as to why you walked away. You'll be amazed at the power and the confidence in just packing up and walking away by saying, not today. If a deal is to be made, you may see an attitude adjustment on your counterpart take place as I have found that people are more motivated by loss than the premise of gain.

So, what's the point? The point is when you walk into a negotiation or dispute resolution you need to be prepared. You need to be sure of what you need and want and have a Plan B and alternatives ready. Do your part in orchestrating a creative atmosphere where all parties in the room can have an open and honest dialogue. Never be afraid to say no and walk away from a bad deal, just do it properly.

SPEAK WITH A SMILE

Growing up, I always heard the phrase, "The world loves winners." Now I initially associated winners with movie stars, athletes, and rich people, and so on. I obviously did not fit into any of those categories, so I asked myself, self, how could I be perceived as a winner when I really don't fit the winner profile? The answer was simple, just act like a winner. I did my best to dress like a winner, albeit on a very low budget. Got a decent haircut and topped it off with a trained yet natural sincere smile. What a novelty. No big expense. No blood sweat and tears. No real achievement but just a pleasant, yet confident countenance to myself. I was a little lucky that I had a natural smile, though I was not fully aware that it would help me in negotiations and communications. It wasn't till I was in a week-long management training course in Detroit that I kind of figured it out. The instructor was a very sought-after national trainer on real estate management and marketing. He was teaching a class of about 30 young managers from some of the largest independent real estate companies in the country. I was a peon from an NH firm, that was one of the smallest in the group, but who cared I was there. At one point, I was asked to give a presentation in front of the whole

FAILED TO NEGOTIATE THE DEAL

class about a case study on some kind of negotiation. When I completed my interpretation and conclusion of the subject matter, the instructor complimented me on the way I proposed to handle the negotiation. Then he said something that I will never forget. He finished his compliment with, "But who can argue with a smile like that?" I was on cloud nine as I had been petrified that I was going to bomb in front of all my peers. From that point on, I did my best to train myself to maintain a confident, genteel smile while communicating and dealing with people. Trust me, it took a lot of discipline, as it is so easy to be distracted and fall into a trap of being distraught.

While working as a Vice President of Marketing for a large development company, I had to deal with the VP of finance in funding my projects. We were about the same age. I was the happy-go-lucky guy and he was more like a grumpy old man. I genuinely thought he believed that was the part he had to play, as the finance guy, but it did not suit him well. I swear it reflected badly on his performance and ability to communicate with staff and vendors. One day, feeling a little mischievous, I walked into his office. They're sat grumpy old Richard. I asked him how he was doing. He snarled back, "I am OK." I looked back at him with his sourpuss face and said if you're OK maybe you should notify your face because there seems to be a disconnect there. He snapped back at me, "What the hell do you mean by that?" I said, "Richard you're a bright, talented guy, but you walk around the office like you're pissed off all of the time and nobody is comfortable dealing with you, let alone being open and honest with you. Personally, I don't get it." He paused and took a deep breath and said, "I have to be honest with you, my wife and I are not getting along and my kids are driving me crazy and my home life is in shambles and it is obvious that I am bringing my personal problems to the office." I told him I was sorry to hear that and I asked if there was anything I could do to help. He said that just being able to talk with me in confidence was very helpful. I said Richard, you have two problems, one, your home life is in trouble, and two, you're bringing it to work. Maybe I can help you with the second problem, which may, in turn, help you at home. I explained to him that everyone loves a winner spiel that starts with a simple sincere smile. He looked at me with a little crinkle of a smile and said, "You know, that makes sense. I have always watched you walk around the office smiling and telling stories and everybody seems to like and feel comfortable dealing with you, and honestly, it made me a little jealous." I said, "Here's the deal, from now on when you walk into your office you not only flip on the light switch, you turn on your smile switch. You have a choice; your office, like your personality, can be dark or bright, happy or sad. My suggestion, turn them both on... period. I want you to pretend that there is a video camera filming you speaking with people or talking on the phone, and in front of you, create a little note card that says Speak with a Smile. Go even further, walk with a smile, text with a smile, and email with a smile. If you're still in the dumps, think of something that made you smile, made you laugh, or made you happy. The bottom line is to look happy even though you may have to pretend or work at it." I asked Richard to develop his smile routine and notice the reaction from his coworkers and business partners. I even started singing the song "When you're smiling, the whole world smiles with you," by Louis Armstrong. Richard was fully receptive to my suggestions and very diligent in employing the smiling switch. Weeks later, he asked me into his office and thanked me for my candor and guidance, and said his new routine was making a difference. He said, "Sometimes I think I am actually a funny guy and have been known to make people laugh, and you know what, that makes me happy." He continued, I come to work, turn on the light switch, turn on the smile switch, and enjoy dealing with people for a change. Best of all, when I leave work, I shut off the light switch, but keep my smile switched on, and when I get home it's infectious. I didn't realize that I was the one that set the bar for grumpiness and I now have the ability to change that bar to happiness... "the whole world smiles with you."

I have proven to myself over and over again that when I am negotiating or communicating when I am happy and smiling versus when I am sick, angry, or tired the outcomes are quite different. The benefits of being a happy-go-lucky person are overwhelming. It's amazing how a confident smile and a genuine expression of care builds trust, expands relationships, tears down one's natural defensive shields, and gets to the truth... their needs, wants, and urgencies. In negotiations, you have to have the ability to open people up and let them speak freely, and listen to them with an empathetic smile.

So, what's the point? The point is that everyone loves a winner. The definition of a winner is broad. In my case, a sincerely caring person, that speaks with a smile and is able to communicate with people in a fun, non-combative way is a winner. It's a process that can be infectious for your counterpart. For when someone senses that you're not there to beat them up, a sigh of relief will overcome them and create an environment that can build trust, a healthy relationship, and get the problem solved. I remember one time after I negotiated a tough deal for one of my clients, they asked me how I was able to deal with my difficult counterpart, I simply said, "Easy, we like each other."

"LISTEN, YAH, YAH, YAH, DO YOU WANT TO KNOW A SECRET? YAH, YAH, YAH"

Growing up, the Beatles were my favorite band. It seems like they wrote a new song every week. Sometimes those songs and others would resonate with me about real-life issues and experiences where I was personally weak. When I knew I was in trouble communicating a message, I would recite this song to myself to slow down, shut up, retool, and listen. The craft of being a good listener is one of the most important tools that you can have in your negotiation/communications repertoire. The challenge is that a very high percentage of us are not good listeners, pure and simple. The first thing you need to do to achieve listening greatness is to buy into the concept that this skill will be one of your most important skills. The second thing you need to do is acknowledge that your listening skills are subpar. The third thing you need to do is train for this skill daily and never stop. Finally, if you get in trouble, sing the Beatles song to yourself and want to know their secrets, which is what their real needs and wants are. Just remember, for most of us, listening is not a natural process and requires a lot of effort. It has been said there is nothing worse than a lousy listener, but there is, they're called the interrupter. These folks not only are terrible at listening, but they interrupt, interject, and generally mess up the whole conversation. This typically increases tension in the negotiation and delays or ruins a good outcome.

Many times, I've used the phrase "it's all about them." Meaning that I want to focus on them rather than having them hear about me. In many cases, they could care less about me. They want to be heard and be able to tell their story, which is what you should want.

I remember hearing the story about a businessman that is at a networking group and approaches another guy that he feels would be a good business contact. He makes the initial introduction and starts talking to the guy and explains who he is, what his job is, where he went to school, what kind of fancy cars and boats he has, that he is a spectacular tennis player, and on and on thinking he is going to impress his newfound friend. This supposedly newfound friend just shakes his hand, remains quiet, and says it was nice to meet you, but I must move on. As he walks away, he says to himself what a big mouth, know it all. I hope I never have to do business with him. Sensing that this approach was not well received the guy retools and goes back to the networking group and seeks out another person to connect with. He makes his introduction and asks him about his job and listens. Then he asks where he lives and listens. Then he asks about his family and listens. Then asks him what he likes to do in his free time and listens and so on. At the end of the conversation, they shake hands and both say it was nice to meet you. While the new connection walks away, he is thinking to himself what a great guy. He is the type of person I would like to do business with.

The benefits of being a great listener are huge. Being quiet or pausing and listening gives your counterpart a comfortable opportunity to blow off some steam, vent, and release any anger holed up inside of them with the desired result being, "Now that I got that off my chest, we can move on." It also creates an environment where your counterpart can participate in a free flow of ideas and a sense of inclusion. This in turn helps determine their needs, wants, urgencies, and what motivates them. Best of all it creates a space where you all can have ownership in solving a problem or negotiation, where everyone at the table can feel they contributed and were heard. The bottom line is, keep them talking. I have always said, I can deal with the known; however, I cannot deal with the unknown. Keeping them talking while being a good listener solves that dilemma. After all, the more information, the better the decision.

Asking key questions is the answer to the listening problem. Keep them short and sweet and give them plenty of time to answer. Don't be afraid to ask for clarification; the last thing you want to do is misinterpret the message they are trying to convey. Asking questions like, I am not sure? I don't fully understand what you mean? Could you elaborate please? It is not a display of ignorance on your part, but shows that you are a good listener and that you care about understanding their message. The wise negotiator needs to fully appreciate that people want and deserve to be heard, respected, and understood, it's that simple. The idea of being overbearing and talking over someone is not the right approach for gaining the trust and gaining the honest truth from your counterpart. Without honest and clear answers, you'll need to be a great interpreter or psychoanalysis, which can be dangerous. In my experience, people sometimes say what they don't mean and you have to have the ability to determine whether it's an honest answer, an emotional response, or one filled with deceit. Being a great communicator is a little like the chicken and egg theory. What comes first? Being a great speaker or a great listener? My bet, speak less and listen more.

So, what's the point? The point is, being a sincere, careful listener is vital to having a productive conversation accompanied by thoughtful questions. It may not come naturally, so it's important to stay focused on the benefits of being quiet and allowing your counterpart to talk and tell you their story, not just some of their story, but their whole story, only then can you deal with their real problems. The master listener is not only a great listener for what is being said, but is able to feel and interpret what is not being said.

PUSH, DON'T SHOVE...

As strange as it sounds, some people cannot make a decision. You may be a great negotiator, but if you can't get them to sign on the bottom line, it's all for naught. I can tell you firsthand how frustrating it is to do your diligence, negotiate in good faith, have a meeting of the minds, and still, no commitment. You can shake your head and give up or you navigate carefully forward. For me, giving up was never an option. When people want something, but don't really need it, that can be the bigger issue. A few years back I was looking to buy a boat. I had a small, older Boston Whaler but wanted to get a newer, bigger one. The local dealer had a left-over boat from the previous year which was perfect and it was priced right. I spoke to the salesperson and he convinced me that the boat was priced right and the only thing I needed to negotiate was extras, like dock lines and fenders, etc. To sweeten the deal, Boston Whaler was offering a $1,500 rebate that ended in 3 days. The salesperson was reasonably laid back, clearly not the aggressive type. I told him that I would think about it and get back to him. He did remind me on the way out that the rebate ended shortly. I wanted the boat, but didn't need the boat and could not make a decision. I did what most people do and took the path of least resistance by doing nothing. For the next several days I struggled with whether I should buy that dumb-ass boat or not until I procrastinated long enough for the rebate to expire. I did not buy the boat but was disappointed that the salesperson did not follow up with me to remind me of three things: The boat was still available, it was priced right, and the $1,500 rebate was a no-brainer decision. No hard sell, just the facts and a follow-up. I simply needed a gentle push to get me off the fence and make the deal. My experience is that people need to be pushed a little, or maybe a better word to be guided. The fine line, which really is dependent on who you're dealing with, is how to implement the push strategy without shoving or being too aggressive. It's a balancing act. Too aggressive and your counterpart could interpret it in a number of ways. They may sense that you are desperate for a sale and don't have their interests in mind or on the flip side if you don't give them a gentle push, they will not make a decision. I've found over the years that the best practice is to understand that it's natural for people to procrastinate and it's my job to help them make a decision. How I do it depends on their personality. I just keep the conversation going, do reasonable follow-up, and keep asking questions. I know If I stop the follow-up, there is a good chance the deal will die. I always maintain that if I ignore the negative noise and focus on the positive points, keep the train moving, eventually we will figure it out and reach a deal. I just want to be the train's engine, not its caboose.

Years ago, when I was working with a large development group, one of my responsibilities was land acquisitions. I found a gorgeous piece of land that was in a town that was considered a suburb of Boston. The property was about 75 acres and it was an old apple tree farm that had been in a family for four generations. The current owners basically had given up on farming the trees, knowing that the land was far more valuable than an apple orchard. It was for sale by the owner, so I would be dealing with the owners directly, which was fine by me. I met with the owners and I explained that we wanted to build high-end well-designed single-family homes on the land. They were okay with that. They explained their price and suggested terms to do a deal. After a few weeks of negotiations, or what they called a conversation, we came up with a price, terms, and conditions that were acceptable to both sides. In theory, we were both happy with the verbal proposed deal. I told them I would have our legal team draw up a purchase and sales agreement to memorialize the deal in writing and have it to them in a week. Like clockwork, I had the written offer to them for their signature. The sellers were a brother and sister. The brother told me to drop off the paperwork at his house and give them a day to review it. By the end of the next day, I had not heard from them, so I gave the brother a call. I asked if he had any questions. "Nope, I still need more time to look things over," he said. "No problem, I will call you tomorrow." The next day, nothing. By the fourth day, I was getting a little nervous and anxious, but I knew I had to be slow and careful with these folks, as they were clearly people who did not want to be shoved. On the fifth day, I called the brother and asked if the agreement was signed and ready to be picked up. He said no and there was a problem. His sister was going through an emotional meltdown and did not want to sell the property. Ugh, I said to myself, seller's remorse. I asked if there was anything in the agreement that his sister didn't agree with. "No, she just doesn't want to let the property go right now. You have been very good to deal with, so we decided to reimburse you your legal fees as a way of saying sorry for wasting your time." I could have shaken his hand, sent him our legal bill, called it a day, and moved on, but I chose not to. I knew from experience that folks have trouble making up their minds and it was my job to push or guide them a little to try to make sense of it all. I asked the brother if I could meet with them to talk things over one final time with zero pressure. Surprisingly, they agreed and we met. I said to the sister,

"Is there anything in the agreement that upsets you?" "No." "Is there anything that I did or said that bothers you?" "No." "Can I ask you why you changed your mind?" She answered that the property has been Woodmont Farms for over 60 years and it's hard to see it go away. I said that's an easy fix, our marketing department always struggles to name a development. I think Woodmont Farms would be a wonderful name for this community. Boy, did her eyes light up. I said we can go a couple of steps further. If you would like, you could join in making decisions on street names, streetscapes, and the overall theme. "We have a deal," she said.

So, what's the point? The point is people are human and sometimes they need a little friendly push to get them going and to point them in the right direction. Decisions are difficult for a lot of people and they need help. It's our job to keep the conversation going and keep the parties engaged and involved. I am of the belief that through proper dialogue and follow-up, we all can come to terms with a mutually acceptable agreement. Sometimes it takes a little longer than we wished, but that's all about patience. Where there is a will, there is a way.

BUT WHY...

I have a used lot of quirky phrases throughout my career, but in this chapter, the ones I feel most applicable are, "I can't fix if I don't know its broken," or "I can deal with the known but not the unknown," or "Well, why didn't you tell me," or the simple one... "Thanks for asking."

The saying ask and thou shall receive is something that I have lived by. It has helped me in so many ways. The sincere question "Why" is such a huge yet simple one for helping to solve a conflict or to further a negotiation. "Why" is the great motivator. Your job is to unlock the private door of your counterpart or client's mindset and get their honest answer.

Getting the real answer to why is not easy, as the honest answer is sometimes confidential, embarrassing, private, vulnerable, or keeping honest answers to themselves, for fear of it being used or taking advantage of them.

The key to getting honest answers to why is doing your best to get your counterpart, client, or whoever you're dealing with into their comfort zone by creating trust, relationship, and rapport.

I once dealt with a couple that I helped sell their unique ocean view home. It took some doing, but I finally got it sold. They wanted a bigger home inland a bit and at the time there was nothing on the market that fit their needs, so I hooked them up with a rental for 6 months with the option to extend if needed. A couple of months later the perfect home came on the market in their price range. I immediately called the listing broker, who was a friend of mine, and asked for a showing. She surprisingly said she was not able to show it for a week as the sellers were doing some last-minute touch-ups to make the home more presentable. I said to myself, why the heck did she put it in the MLS if it's not ready to show? Oh well. She promised to call me when it was ready to show in the order of the requests she'd received. I was number two. A week later, I got the call. She said her first showing was the next day at 10:00 a.m., so I asked to see it right after that at 11:00. Now the four top questions asked by buyers are, "Why are they selling" "How long has it been on the market" "Have they had any offers" and "What will they take." So, I took the liberty of asking the agent, "Why are they selling?" The agent said the sellers were elderly and wanted to move to Florida. That made sense to me, as the day before we'd had a nasty ice storm and I fell on my ass trying to get into someone else's house on a black icy driveway. Florida sounds good to me then. My clients and I arrived there just before 11:00. and the first buyers were leaving with smiles on their faces... not good. Finally, we went in, and the home, location, and views were absolutely perfect for my buyers. Best of all, it was priced at $865,000, well below market value in my mind. We left the home and my buyers wanted to go back to my office in the afternoon and write up an offer. Meanwhile, I had to call the listing agent and ask some questions so I could draw up a purchase and sales agreement. The listing agent then tells me she has 12 showings lined up and asks if I think she'd underpriced it? Well, I said, it's a snowy cold December and you have 12 showing and possibly multiple offers coming, maybe you priced it perfectly.

At my office with my buyers, I get a call from the listing agent that she has received multiple offers and I would be wise to present an offer over the asking price. Well, that did not sit well with my buyers. After a back and forth with the husband who wanted to make an offer below asking, and the wife who wanted to offer over the asking, they compromised and came in at full asking price and an all-cash deal. I called the listing agent and told her I wanted to present the offer to her buyers; she said no as they were elderly and I could just hand-deliver it to her, which I did. The next day I called the agent for an update. She said they had four offers and the sellers can't make up their mind what to do. Now I knew why they were selling, but I didn't know why they couldn't make up their mind as to which offer to take or whether to counteroffer. So, I said to the listing agent sincerely, my clients love the house, they came in at your full asking price and they are cash buyers; I don't understand what the difficulty is? She said that all the offers were asking for 45 to 60 days to close and that was freaking her sellers out, as they had not found a place in Florida suitable for them... Bingo! I said I would get back to her with another proposal. I immediately met with my buyers and we re-wrote the agreement with a closing date of 60 days or less from the notice that the sellers had found suitable housing, not to exceed nine months. The sellers now had a full price, cash offer, and plenty of time to find their new home. They signed the agreement... Oh, the power of why.

Another Why?

I had an agent that had worked for our real estate agency for many years, who not only generated a reasonable number of sales but was also a great person and a huge asset to our company. She would walk in the office, greet everyone with a smile, go right to her office and get to work. No drama, no issues, just steady Eddie. One day, she walked into my office and asked me if I had a minute to talk. I said sure, come on in. She sat down in front of me, a little teary-eyed, and told me she was leaving us for another agency and she would be clearing out her office tomorrow. I was shocked. I asked her why? She explained that she'd given it a lot of thought and had concluded that she needed a change. She did not want to elaborate, as she had made her final decision. She thanked me, hugged me, and left. I was dumbfounded, sad, and felt like a deer in a headlight.

Our real estate agency was not your traditional agency, as we only hired full-time, experienced agents. The compensation program was also different. We charged a desk fee; any business and personal expenses and the agent would get a monthly bill between $1,400 and $2,000 in return for a 95% split on all their commissions earned. Most other agencies worked solely on a negotiated split with little or no monthly bill; however, their splits would be significantly lower than what we offer.

That evening, sulking in my office, I decided to call her and say a proper goodbye than what I'd experienced at the office. We talked about the camaraderie within the office, our exceptional staff, and all of the fun parties and events we had. At one point during the conversation, I found the opportunity to ask her an important question. Pam, why are you really leaving our company? She paused, hesitated, and slowly went on to tell me that her husband had recently been laid off from his job and they were worried sick about her monthly agency bills and she'd been too embarrassed to explain this to me. A sensation of joy overwhelmed me. I said Pam, I can put you on a similar, if not better split, then you're being offered with no monthly fees, and should you want to switch back in the future, no problem. I knew it was impossible to see her smile over the phone, but I did. She was happy, I was ecstatic, and she stayed with our company. The sincere power of Why.

So, what's the point?

Sometimes people will say things that they don't mean, not in a malicious way, but in a self-protective way. Your job in a negotiation or conflict resolution is to try to get to the honest why of their personal situation. As I mentioned before, it's easy to deal with the known, but very difficult to deal with the unknown. Putting people at ease, building an honest rapport and relationship with folks will open the door and allow different interests and options to flow with mutually beneficial results. Be sincere and ask for the honest "Why."

REJECTION 101

In my younger days, I found it hard to believe how there was no shortage of people who disagreed with me. They rejected my ideas; the young ladies rejected my advances and it was a little confusing. I thought of myself as a smart, cute kid (I must define a cute kid versus a handsome kid... big difference, which was not in my favor). I was somewhat fortunate to be able to take rejection well, as I believed it was natural that not everyone would be on the same page as me. The more experience I received dealing with people, the better I got at it. I convinced myself that rejection or disagreement was nothing more than a second opinion. So, when I got a little pushback, rejection, or a big fat no, I trained myself to pause and ask myself, who is right and who is wrong? Maybe they have a point. Maybe I am wrong. Let's dig deeper. For me, that was the beginning of the art of dealing with negative feedback.

I remember when I got my first business card, I was very excited that I was so important that I had to have a business card. I was very experienced in new home construction, as my dad sold doors, windows, and trim boards to builders. On weekends I would hang around with him and help measure rough openings and lineal footage for trim and baseboards. I felt very comfortable dealing with builders. My first business rejection came early, as in my first day on the job. I drove by a home under construction and saw a for sale by builder sign. This was a spec home, meaning that the builder was building it on speculation that they would eventually find a buyer. No real estate agent was involved either, as he was trying to save a commission. I drove down the muddy driveway and figured out who the builder was. I approached him saying, "Hi there, you have a great house here, and what a great location." I introduced myself as an agent that specialized in new construction and asked him if he needed any help in selling the home. Nope, I can sell it on my own, I don't need a "realta." I must have caught him finishing up his morning break, as he was eating a muffin and drinking coffee while he was talking to me. At that point, I took out one of my brand-new business cards, handed it to him, and said, "If you need any help selling, please give me a call." He took the card, looked at it for a few seconds, then abruptly tore it in half and started to clean his teeth with it. I paused, looked at him with his shit-eating grin, and like John Wayne, I pulled out another card and handed it to him. Here is another one for lunch and I walked away.

I quickly figured out that sales or deal-making is just a numbers game. In order to get to a "yes," I would have to deal with a series of no's; it was all about persistence and not taking rejection personally.

When I was the owner/broker of a real estate company, in theory, I was in the real estate business, but in actuality, I was in the agent recruiting business. Recruit and retain was my motto, and it was not easy. Rejection came quickly and often. I dreaded the calls to agents to have lunch or a sit down with me about joining our company. In the beginning, it did not go well. I heard every excuse known to mankind for why they would not meet with me, never mind joining my company. Frustrated, yes, but I understood the value of persistence and the numbers game. Don't get me wrong, I had success with recruiting agents, but the numbers were way too high with the ratio from no to yes. The only thing I could do was make more calls, which at that point was not a big deal. I had my systems and dialogue down pat and went at it with a healthy attitude. Still, my rejection rate was way too high. Something had to give. I had this old saying that became very useful to me, not only in business but in life. If I was doing something that ended with poor, undesirable results, maybe I was doing it wrong. The proof is in the pudding and with such a dismal conversion rate on my recruiting efforts, maybe I was doing it wrong and needed to develop a new approach. I gave it a lot of thought and figured out that the most common objection from my targeted recruits was that they were happy where they were and it would be a waste of time to meet. Okay, time for a new approach. I did a 180 and developed a whole new approach on the premise that my targets were happy where they were. I would call and ask if they would like to meet so we could get to know each other and they could hear what our firm had to offer. I acknowledged that I knew they were happy where they were; however, I simply wanted to be their next choice, if anything should change. Most agents are loyal, but also curious. They like to feel like they are wanted. So, the approach to soft-sell the appointment and get them to meet with me gave me the opportunity to plant the seed for the future. My gamble was that if something happened at their office, like a new manager, office policy, or some other significant change, I was their Plan B. It worked, and my conversion rate doubled.

So, what's the point? The point is that rejection is part of the deal and a natural sequence to deal-making and negotiations. Rejection is a human experience, and how you deal with it sets people apart. You can choose to let it get you down as a personal setback and crawl into a hole or you can choose to simply brush it off and try again with a new approach. I live with the concept that without objections, you're without interest and rejections are simply a hurdle and there may still be interest within. The bottom line is to always have persistence as a passion.

RULE 51

I am not much of a TV person, but I do watch and enjoy the *NCIS* series. NCIS stands for the Naval Criminal Investigation Service. On the show, they do a lot of high-action national security investigations. On one show they were dealing with a major computing hack that would create panic and chaos in the Washington D.C. area. The leader of the NCIS team is Mark Harmon, AKA Gibbs, a cool, calm, very capable, no-nonsense leader. He has two subordinates on the team. McGee, who is one serious guy and all business, and Dinozzo, who is a fun-loving, cocky but confident agent. In this particular episode, McGee is distracted from his work, dealing with his family, as his dad is seriously ill. While the computer hackers are causing a meltdown in the D.C. area, Gibbs decides to enlist the help of three convicted computer hackers and release them from prison to help track down the bad guys. Once in custody at NCIS, McGee and Dinozzo interrogate the prisoners, and for whatever reason are not able to get any useful information. McGee, totally stressed out with his family issues, feels as though these three guys are jerking everyone around and screams this is a waste of time. He wants to send them back to prison. Gibbs goes in, separates the three, and does his Cool Hand Luke personality. He eventually gets some useful information out of one of the guys. Gibbs then asks McGee to go back in again and drill them separately. McGee flips out and says that they won't help, they're simply playing them. He refuses to go back in for another interrogation. Gibbs, who is the boss, and is not someone you say no to, plays by a set of rules that he assigns numbers to. He looks at McGee with his piercing eyes and says strongly, "Rule 51." McGee sheepishly asks him what is Rule 51? Gibbs takes out a piece of paper and writes down on one side Rule 51 and on the other side he writes down, "SOMETIMES YOU'RE WRONG." McGee pauses, takes a deep breath, grabs the file, mentally retools, and goes back into the interrogation room. With a new attitude and a fresh approach, he's able to isolate one of the convicts and manages to get enough information to be able to track down the hackers. In the end, NCIS saves the day and all ends well.

Rule 51, is a rule that we should all recognize, respect, and remind ourselves, that yes, sometimes we're wrong. I know that in the past I personally got stuck on a position or an argument that I was so convinced I was right that I was not flexible. In those cases, things didn't go well. Finally, when enough people said to me that I was wrong, common sense would prevail and I'd admit I was wrong and retooled. Sometimes, human nature dictates that we do not want to acknowledge making a mistake, which tends to lead us down a dead-end road. In negotiations and deal-making, the Rule 51 folks are not afraid of admitting being wrong, taking a hit, and moving on. When I ran my real estate company, at one point we were doing over 700 transactions a year. With that type of volume, there are bound to be mistakes and there were. My policy to my agents was that if a major issue or lawsuit was about to surface, I would back them 100 percent. If we determined that the cause was our mistake, then we would fess up quickly and try to remediate the problem ASAP. I believe having the ability to recognize that you are wrong, made a mistake, or simply, going in the wrong direction is the trait of a smart negotiator. I am sure your counterpart would be pleasantly surprised at your candor and sincerity when you simply say, oops, I screwed up, sorry, let's move on. One of my favorite lines to a lawyer when I was bailing out one of my agents who was promising the moon was that my agent made a verbal typo, we're sorry. That lawyer almost pissed his pants laughing and gave us a pass.

So, what's the point? The point is that honesty is your best policy and having the ability to admit a mistake sooner rather than later is the right thing to do. If you continue to defend your mistake it only makes your counterpart distrust you more. If you admit you're wrong and retool, your counterpart will reward you with respect. The process of, as they say, stopping the bleeding by taking your lumps and without missing a beat moving on to focus on your goal and desired outcome is a great personal asset.

NEVER LET THE ENEMY KNOW
THEY'RE THE ENEMY

I have a buddy of mine who claims Greek heritage. He once told me that there was an old Greek saying, "Never let the enemy know they're the enemy." I thought I had heard them all, but this phrase was a new one, a little complicated, yet worth digging deeper. After some thoughts and reflections on some of my past negotiations that had less than desirable outcomes, its meaning hit me. To me, it is a personal strategy to not let your negotiation counterpart know that you have a personal distrust, dislike, or any negative feelings toward them. Before I understood the concept, there were times that I would not hold back my true feelings toward my counterpart. Quickly and invariably the negotiation would become more tense and difficult to complete.

I remember when George W. Bush, as President, announced that Iran, Iraq, and North Korea were the axis of evil. When I heard that, I said to myself that was a bold and threatening statement, not that they weren't though. Think about it, President Bush just announced to the world that basically, he dislikes, does not trust, and has labeled these three countries as evil. What did he accomplish by those statements? Did it make him look tough? Scare those nations? Make our world a little safer? I say no.

What I believe really happened is that he put them on notice that there is no trust or friendship or chance for a better relationship between the U.S. and these three countries. Even worse, they went rogue and nuclear programs continued as well as death to America chants and rallies. This taught me that the Greek saying was true and I therefore would do my best to keep my opinions and dislikes to myself regarding my counterpart, and only continue the negotiations with a cautious eye.

Years ago, I was involved in a significant commercial real estate transaction involving a listing broker who had a horrible reputation. I'd never experienced it first hand, but enough of my colleagues had told me to watch my back. With this head up from my friends, I continued with respect and professionalism in my approach in dealing with him. Right from the start his true colors, as warned, started to show. He became evasive with pertinent information, lied about facts and when we finally had a verbal agreement, he stalled the signing of the purchase agreement, only to find out that he was shopping my deal to his own buyers. When I figured out his motives, my first instinct was to go ballistic and call him out on his lying and his lack of trust. Fortunately, the Greek saying came to mind and told me to stop, don't let him know that I know he can't be trusted. I have a client that I need to serve and protect, and any tension or volatility could jeopardize the deal. Now knowing how this person fully operates, I reverified all of his information and put a full-court press on getting the final purchase agreement signed and delivered... all with a smile. In the end, the property closed without incident. My client was very happy with the property and was not aware of the tension that existed with the other agent or the transaction. For me, it was a personal accomplishment of emotional control and playing a deceitful counterpart.

So, what's the point? The point is that it is not productive in a negotiation or a relationship to go off the deep end and let your counterpart have it, even though you could be justified by their behavior. If you do, expect a counterpunch, and their defense shield will surface. Future deals and negotiations will be difficult. The correct approach is to grin and bear it and plot forward knowing there will be difficult obstacles. Take full charge of the situation, don't expect full cooperation with your counterpart, but by all means, protect the deal.

THE TAIL OF
TWO STRAWS

We have always heard the phrase "The straw that broke the Camel's back." Well, I have experienced this first hand in dealing with people. But I have to go one step further, as I have discovered two straws, the good straw, and the bad straw. Sometimes it's all about the little things in life and when they add up, there becomes a so-called tipping point that may be good or bad. Knowing and understanding the concept and value of the tipping point can help you deal effectively with people, whether you're the cause or there were outside influences to tip the scales as a seesaw.

The bad straw is when the person you're dealing with hits a boiling point and goes off the chart mad. In some cases, it could be one simple statement from you or who you're negotiating on behalf of that sets them off, but in most cases, it's something gnawing at someone or what I call ankle-biting with dribbling of bad news or statements contrary to what the person believes or wants. Most people are decent and will take a jab here and there, but when they add up, BOOM and all hell breaks loose. For those that don't understand the tipping point, they ask, "What just happened?" Why are they freaking out over such a small little issue? The truth is, it's not that issue alone, but the culmination of many issues that added up to a breaking point.

I had an agent that worked for our real estate company. She was an amazing woman. Trained as an executive secretary who then got into real estate sales and nailed it! She was polished, well-spoken, knew the business well, and was one of the most professional agents I've ever worked with. On one occasion, she was working on behalf of a local CEO and selling a multi-million-dollar new construction home. I personally knew the builder who was famous for his arrogance. As the transaction progressed, I made the mistake of asking her how the deal was going. She responded lousy, the builder is a jerk to deal with, but we will get through it. The next week, she stopped by my office for some advice and brought up how the builder was nickel and diming her client. Once again, however, she smiled and said we will get through it. A few days later she came into my office and explained the builder was relentless on his demands and had been extremely condescending to her. She added that she had really nice clients and we will get through it. Fast forward a couple of days and boom, my office door flies open and my cool, calm professional agent looks like Cruella Deville. She says, I have had it with this asshole builder and I'm about to tell him to take a hike and take this contract and shove it up his butt. For those who knew the old Maxell Tape commercial, it was like this giant audio speaker was pointed right at me as I sat in my chair and turned on full volume as my hair, cheeks, mouth, and lips were blown backward and trembling. Once her volume lowered, I asked her what happened. She said that the builder had the gall to ask for a $100,000 non-refundable deposit from her client. I said to myself, honestly, that's a reasonable request on a custom-built multi-Million-dollar home and she should have known that. My mind was racing to figure out how to react as she continued to rant on about the builder. My concerns were losing a huge deal, maybe losing a client, or worse, losing my agent who had just cracked her tipping point. I had two choices, fuel the fire and throw the builder under the bus and support her meltdown or let her vent, listen, then calm her down. I chose wisely to let her vent and blow off some steam. I didn't interrupt. I listened to her story for as long as she needed. After about an hour of ripping the builder, she ran out of anger and she looked at me and said, "Do you think I am taking this too personally?" I calmly told her that she was passionate about representing her clients and it showed. This builder had a reputation for being a high-quality builder however; he was also known to lack people skills and that's where she excels. She paused for a minute and looked at me with an innocent smile and said, "You're right, I am the professional and we will get through this, thanks for listening."

The good straw is your friend. It's the type of tipping point that tends to get people off the fence and to a decision. I liken it to being an influencer. Something that persuades people as a motivator or creates urgency. I learned rather quickly that people tend to procrastinate and put off making decisions and committing. For me, this was always a mystery. My DNA is to make decisions, get them off my plate, and move on. My wife always used to make fun of me for making hasty decisions that did not always work out. I rationalized them by saying, if I am not making mistakes, I am not moving forward. You learn from mistakes and with that, I had a great education. My goal with the tipping point concept was to try to change people's minds or get them to make a decision favorably to what I was selling.

When I ran my real estate office, on the surface I was in the real estate business, but really, I was in the agent business. My main job was recruiting experienced agents. Recruiting was no different from regular sales as if I had a product to sell. The product I was trying to sell was myself and our company. I always would adhere to Marketing 101, 4 Ps: Product, place, promotion, and price. Product was our brick and mortar, staff, management, and training. Place was the location of our office. Promotion was our marketing and internet presence. Price was their commissions split. Easy enough... not. I knew my product and I developed a targeted audience, created a contact management system to consistently reach out to my sphere, and ask them if they would like to get together and learn about our company. Their answers were like a broken record; No thank you, I am happy where I am. It's very easy to get discouraged in sales; however, it's all about persistence and counting the No's. Meaning, how many No's does it take to get a yes. Once I figured out that ratio, it would motivate me to make all the calls I needed to get more Yes's. The next step was to lower the No's ratio by getting them to change their minds by finding their tipping point, the point they say yes. I would build a relationship with them by consistently reaching out to them and asking how their business was going and how their family was doing. I was amazed by the fact that over time, they would share with me the grievances they had with their current company and how they were being treated. I would hang up the phone and say to myself, the timing is not now, but I've just added ten pounds to the seesaw. In time, I would learn that there was a common denominator of grievances and if I countered them and offered them a better solution, I would tip them over and get them to change their mind and make the decision I wanted. I heard the same complaints consistently, commission splits were low, I don't feel appreciated, I have competing managers, our marketing is horrible, or the worst, our office is becoming toxic. Persistence and patience are a virtue and if I continued to reach out to them gently, it would only be a matter of time before they hit their tipping point. That is, I need a change and your company is the answer. I basically wanted to position myself as their Plan B when they reached their tipping point.

The good straw is a cool concept that is effective with people who have trouble making decisions or commitments. You basically build a rapport with whom you're dealing with, figure out their needs, wants, and urgencies and develop a drip campaign, which is a slow, methodical process of listening to their concerns and providing them with solutions for how you can make their situation better. You have to be consistent and persistent. It may take some time, but your goal is that after each conversation, or whatever method of communication you choose, you're adding a little weight to their mental seesaw. It's hard to figure out how much weight you will need to tip them over, but again, it's all about persistence.

So, what is the point? The point is understanding the concept and value of the tipping point gives you an advantage in dealing with people. When the ugly straw raises its head and your client, counterpart, or even a friend or neighbor goes off the chart unexplainably mad, your first thought may be to engage their anger or fight and defend yourself or your position. The correct response is, however, to let them blow, spill their guts, and listen to them with compassion and empathy. Once they start to calm down, let them know that you understand what they're saying, but be sure to also ask them what else is bothering them. Give them the opportunity to tell you what is really bothering them. It may simply be a lot of small issues that add up to one big issue. Once you identify their real concerns, only then will you be able to deal with them effectively.

The good straw is a mental process that contributes to helping someone make a decision. Dealing with people is what I call a contact sport. You need to develop a slow consistent approach to communications, offer pertinent information, provide valuable feedback, maintain the relationship and be patient. The goal is to tip the yes scale.

BULLS, LIONS, TIGERS, AND BEARS... OH MY

One of the biggest challenges in negotiations and quite frankly, everything is about dealing with people. Of the many things that I have learned over the years is that you can be the best negotiator in the world, be the best-trained salesperson, but if you can't deal with people, you're severely handicapped. I came to realize at an early age that there are various types of people out there and the quicker I recognize that, the quicker I can adjust my approach and try to build a relationship. There are the bulls in the china cabinet and the lions and tigers that come at you with their claws. On the flip side, there are the soft-spoken folks who like calm. The engineers who want facts. The accountants who want numbers. I found that trying to analyze their personality types upfront helped me to categorize them into my box of quadrants, meaning a box that is divided into four different personality groups. Namely, folks that like to deal calmly and quietly, folks who dwell on the facts and details, folks who are hard charges and big talkers, folks who simply want a good relationship and fairness. We could go on and on about the different personality types, but the point is that you have to figure out what type of person you're dealing with and adjust your approach to their personality. I sometimes refer to this being a good chameleon. You figure out what type of person they are, adjust to their personality, and start to build a rapport and a relationship. Once you feel comfortable with the relationship, you can slowly adjust your personality to be yourself.

I used to teach a sales class. My favorite segment was the discussion on dealing with people. I would start the program by saying, "People like to deal with people like themselves," then we would talk about personality types and how to figure them out. I suggested that when you meet people for the first time, start off very polite, professional, and respectful and let them talk. Then ask questions, but also listen because at this point it's all about them. It's important to get them to talk, talk, talk. If you understand the importance of trying to figure out what type of person they are, you can slowly adjust your style to be more congruent to theirs. Once you've made your personal adjustment and start to bond with them, magic happens. They start to lower their natural defense shields and open up honestly to you. Everyone has a natural defense shield toward salespeople, negotiators, or almost anybody they meet for the first time. Once you're in the honesty zone, it becomes much easier to figure out what is truly their needs, wants, and urgencies. I've always said, "I can deal with the known but I can't deal with the unknown". Once you build a relationship and establish a rapport, only then can you deal effectively with people.

When I was VP of an international construction company, we had many luxury condominium projects in New England under construction. I was responsible for all of the sales and marketing and sometimes would hire outside marketing companies. However, for most of the properties, we had our own in-house sales team. In one particular project in southern New Hampshire, we were having problems staffing the model home. The community was on the high-end side, yet in a rural area, and sales, for a number of reasons, were slow. I decided to hone my sales skills and man the model myself to experience firsthand what the problems were. I remember one day I was out there all by myself. After a couple of hours and a tank full of coffee, a well-to-do older couple came walking through the door. Now being jacked up with all the caffeine and excited to see mankind, I pounced on them like a lion on a goat. I welcomed them to the community and pummeled them with questions, staying with them like a ball on a chain. In a short time, the husband turned to me and said he had seen enough. They asked for a brochure and started off toward their exit. My brain started racing as the perfect buyers for this development were walking out the door and there were few and far between. I quickly came to my senses, and retooled my approach, as they appeared to be a quiet, calm couple. Sincerely I said, "I've had way too much coffee and I think you like the property so I'm just going to sit over there and let you roam around the property without me running my gums. I will be available for questions at any time." The wife laughed and said that she would like to continue to look around and thanked me. Now that I had a good sense of their personality type, I adjusted my approach, slowed down my tempo, and eventually, their defense shields came down and they gave me their needs, wants, and urgencies. It was then easy to see that the property was a perfect fit for them and at this point, it was time to close the deal. We talked about minor changes, interior selections, pricing, and closing dates. All was going well, except for one thing, the wife was hung up on the fact that we did not supply a washer and dryer. I looked at the wife and thanked her for her patience in dealing with a rusty salesman and said that not only would I get her a washer and dryer, but they'll also be Maytag's. She smiled, laughed, and said we have a deal. One may say that this was a little corny; however, being authentic and forthcoming always works for me.

So, what's the point? The point is that everyone has a different personality, as they have their own fingerprint and DNA. The successful negotiator or dealmaker has to understand this and be able to determine what type of person they are dealing with and adjust their own approach and tempo accordingly. The process should be simple. Build a bond, gain trust, lower defense shields, and get to the truth, their needs, wants, and urgencies and deal with them.

WHITE-COLLAR
BULLIES

Growing up I was the target of the schoolyard bullies and why not? I was small, skinny, redheaded, had big teeth, big ears, and came from a poor family. I learned really quickly that bullies were typically big (bigger than me), stupid, kind of ugly, and weren't bright enough to be recognized on their own merits, so they choose instead to be bullies, and that was their temporary rise to fame. My favorite bully was Wayne, AKA Muggzie. He fit my profile, dumb, ugly, and bigger than me. The ugly part came when he was young and he got in a bicycle accident and knocked his two front teeth out. He decided not to fix or replace them because he thought missing those teeth was cool-looking. Well, the Muggster chose me as one of his prime targets and from time to time I would get a mild beating/ humiliation in the schoolyard, local neighborhood, or the worst one, the school locker room. Almost always in front of a somewhat sympathetic audience. I guess in retrospect, it was a good lesson without too much collateral damage that I quickly learned the typical profile of a bully. I learned to shut up, stay clear of them, run like the wind, and eventually got myself a black belt in Karate... end of the schoolyard bullies.

Now fast forward to the business world, gee whiz, they're back. Dumb, ugly, and when I say ugly, I don't necessarily mean in looks, but in persona and demeanor. And now they were dressed for success. They prey on the weak and quiet with their sword of loud, brash, and intimidating behavior. Negotiating with these folks has its challenges. They tend to be ill-informed, loud, and obnoxious and it's my way or the highway type of people. Their strategy is simple, try to ram the deal down your throat, be loud, forceful, and take no prisoners. My lesson learned from Muggzie, once he couldn't beat me up anymore, is to look them straight in the eyes with strength and conviction and say, "That does not work for me. You're going to have to do better than that," without flinching.

I worked with a client that did a fair number of high-end developments in the coastal areas of NH. He was a fun, unique, Ivy League guy that did not fit the profile of a typical real estate developer. He would buy prime parcels of land at market value or above market pricing and develop the land into a high-quality single-family neighborhood. He would spend the extra money on on-site planning, sidewalks, street lamps, protective covenants, and specialty signage. His target market was high-end buyers with their own builders or builders that would buy the lots and build homes on speculation. My job was to market the lots, which was not so easy, as they were always expensive for the area, but worth it.

I was working on one of his smaller subdivisions and had sold all of the lots except one, which was the nicest, but also the most expensive lot. One day, I get a call from Chad, who says he's also a builder and wants to look at the last lot. I get there early and he shows up late. Finally arriving in a big Ford F350 super cab with dually tires and a noisy, smelly diesel. Chad jumps out of the truck and says, "I'm Chad, show me what ya got." He was about 6'2 and looked like an old high school football player. I was polite, professional, and showed him the lot lines, site plan, and gave him an overall view of the development. He then asks with a deep, loud voice, "What's the current price?" I said to myself, Dumbo, it's the same price I quoted you on the phone two hours ago when we talked. I did not say that, however; I told him again the current price. He immediately barked, and "That's too much! Ya going to have to go lower if you want a deal from me." My first thought was Muggzie has grown up and his real name is Chad. I explained to Chad how this was the last lot available, all the other lots had sold at full price, and the seller was firm on his price. He approached me to within three inches from my face and said, "Here's how the deal is going to happen. Your seller is going to knock off $10,000 and you are forgoing your commission from the seller, dropping it down another 5%, then I will do the deal." He then continued, "I will let you list my million-dollar spec home and give you 30 days to sell it, after which I will have my in-house people sell it." I said, "Seriously, you are only giving me 30 days to sell a million-dollar pre-sale to drop my entire commission?" He said, "Ya, you can do it." I looked at him from my 5'10" position, on a good day, and said, "I can't speak for the seller, but there is no way I am dropping my commission and working for you. I will let you know the answer from the seller regarding the $10,000 drop." I said goodbye and left.

I immediately called the seller and told him what had happened. He laughed and said he would not move on the price; it would not be fair to the other folks that paid full price. His response was not surprising, as he was a very fair and honorable person.

I returned to the office with good news, I had a message from a couple that was moving back to the area from California, and their best friend who lived near the area had told them about the lot. They wanted to meet me that night, knowing it was the last lot in that subdivision. I met them there and two hours later the lot was under agreement at full price. I could not wait to pass on the news to Chad Man.

So, what's the point? The point is that you will encounter bullies through-out your career and you will have to deal with them. The best way to deal with these bullies is to be brave and confident, ignore the threats, don't show your feelings, don't bully back, and stay on track with your desired results.

BEING HUMAN,
ONE LEG AT A TIME

I have been very fortunate over the years to work and deal with all sorts of different people. I have always been fascinated with their life stories, trials, tribulations, and success. I was also blessed to work and deal with some very talented people such as Rock Stars, Politicians, Writers, and Successful Business folks. I was never jealous of any of their success, just curious how they achieved their great accomplishments. Coming from a very humble beginning, I was quite uncomfortable with working with people of such a higher social status than me. Although at that time, the bar was really low. Like a fish out of water, I felt that I was clearly out of my league. Awkward, timid, and inferior, I proceeded to work with these folks, but I was not myself. My smile was now serious, my relaxed approach was now stressed, and my confidence had vanished. I am sure that approach had a negative effect on my rapport building, but some of the people were sensitive to my feelings and gave me a pass. After each meeting with these folks, I would go back to my office and mentally review why I would freeze up and act like a puppy trying to please its master. I quickly discovered that I was intimidated by these folks. They were not intimidating me like a bully would, just their successful posture intimidated me. Like the last chapter, I would like to reiterate that bullies are bad, and if not handled properly, they will develop ED, Evil and Destruction. Knowing it was not them, but I, that was the cause of my uneasiness, I did my best to figure out a way to get over my anxiety in working with these people. I found an old saying that "We all put our pants on the same way: One leg at a time" which I interpreted to mean that no one is essentially better or different than anyone else. I lived and breathed by that saying and in time, I treated everyone the same whether it was a carpenter or a Captain of industry, regardless of any social or successful advantage... all the same. It proved to be successful as I treated them all as Kings and Queens and my happy-go-lucky consistent approach worked. I did not allow intimidation to rent space in my head freely.

Living on the Seacoast of NH, there was this cool little restaurant overlooking a first-class marina. It was relatively new and at that time the tourists had not discovered it yet, so it was somewhat quiet and comfortable and a lot of local business people would eat there. They were famous for the Lobster rolls and their towering seafood appetizer platter. The waitstaff were mostly local kids in college and were great at what they did, fun, exciting, and energetic. There was one young lady, who was a senior in a local college, that waited on us a lot. She was an absolute riot, she was fun, pleasant, quick-witted, and full of energy. The food was great, but she made our dining experience exceptional. At that time, I owned a fairly successful real estate company and knew just about everybody in the business arena. From time to time, we would talk about business, as she was majoring in marketing. On one Sunday night, it was a little slow, so she had extra time to talk to us while dealing with other folks. She brought up a discussion of dealing with people and that she was intimidated by working with high-powered people. I said that was amazing to hear because I found her to be so outgoing and sociable. She went on to say that at times she felt insecure and she would freeze up and not be herself. I went on to say that I found that difficult to believe especially how you're handling the patrons here tonight with such grace and ease. She said, what do you mean? I said the table over there sits a current U.S. Senator and his family, on the other side was a gentleman with his family that owns the Marina and a bunch of car dealerships, and off to the left was the CEO of one of the area's largest manufacturing companies and you have handled them with perfection. Her look went from curious to distraught, and like a light switch, her mood and behavior changed. Oh my God, I got to go, she said. Next, she was running around like a mad man trying to please everybody with a nervous and uncomfortable disposition, totally opposite from how she handled these folks just minutes before. My wife looked at me and said, nice job, big mouth. I could not believe my eyes how someone could change so quickly with the curse of the intimidation disease. Watching this newfound frantic person was horrible and I truly felt for her. At one point, she whizzed by and dropped off a huge goblet of wine as a thank you for the so-called heads up. We finished dining and when we started to leave, she came over to me and apologized for not paying much attention to us. I said to her we were fine but you're not. I went on to lecture her that those folks are certainly successful people; however, they are nice folks and just human beings like the rest of us. I went on to tell her that we all put on our pants the same way, one leg at a time, so in the end, they're no more special than you and I. I told her to teach herself to consider everybody as equals, with kindness, and be consistent to all in her behavior and she will conquer any intimidation anxieties. She smiled and said I got it; I will never forget this night. Thanks.

Lastly, when I was young and in my prime and had conquered my intimidation phobia, I was driving to meet this gentleman regarding a potential real estate transaction. I was young and had just bought a Mercedes Benz, That's right, a Benz. It was the entry-level, cheaper model, but it still had the Mercedes star on the hood and I was styling. From our phone conversations, I concluded that he was a wealthy southern gentleman and that this meeting would be interesting. We were to meet at a piece of property that he was looking at to build a commercial office building. I pulled up in my Mercedes and got out and introduced myself. We shook hands and when he looked at my car, he said, nice car. Where I come from, we call that a Palm Beach Volkswagen. I was not sure if that was some kind of slam, if he was trying to intimidate me, or what was going on in his head, but I gave him a big smile and said, fortunately, we're not in Palm Beach, let's go look at some land.

Bada Bing, Bada Boom.

So, what's the point? The point is that intimidators can be a fancy word for bullies and Intimidation can be another word for insecurity. Fortunately, early on, I figured out that we are all humans, and even those highly successful people you meet in person, all dressed for success with great posture and poise are no different than anyone else. Yes, they achieved greatness in their field; however, they still go home and put jeans on, walk the dog, have a beer, and get in their jammies at night. They do not need to be treated any differently and honestly, most folks don't want to be treated any differently. If they sense that you're treating them differently, they will not respect you and will not trust your opinions as being honest, but only to please them instead.

WHAT'S YOUR BLOOD TYPE?

Growing up **I quickly** learned that my attitude is everything and that if I was to be successful, I would need to do my best to maintain a positive attitude. Of course, it's very difficult to consistently maintain a healthy attitude, but I committed myself to constantly trying. I read books and attended seminars. In one book that I read, I found the phrase "Positive thinking brings the advantages I desire." When I get down in the dumps, things aren't going my way, or find myself approaching Mr. Negative, I mentally chant, "Positive thinking brings the advantages I desire," over and over again till I get back my smile and positive self-back. Trust me when I say that I've done this chant thousands of times in my career, as Frank Sinatra would sing, flying Hi in April and shot down in May.... That's Life. The challenge, training, and discipline are to always maintain that healthy attitude and be able to identify quickly when you're going mentally south, then adjust your head fast. The interesting part of all this is how I found it takes more work and effort to be negative than to be positive. Even more interesting to me, when I would allow myself to go negative things around me would collapse, break down, or simply go wrong. I actually started watching people who were going mentally south and the worse they got, the worse their situation got; it was like a self-spiraling downward trend that in some cases was comical to watch.

I once worked part-time in a small manufacturing plant in my hometown when I was in high school. There was this guy, Jean, a French Canadian. English was his second language. He was a foreman in one of our departments. I remember one day when I saw him and he looked really pissed off, so I asked him, "What's bothering you?" It's Dave, he is developing a very poor altitude, and it's really pissing me off. I kind of chuckled to myself as I think he confused the word altitude for attitude, but he was such a nice guy that I would never correct him as I thought it might embarrass him. He made the same error a bunch of times. As I thought about it, maybe he was on to something, that attitude wasn't maintaining a proper altitude, meaning not going low, but staying above the fray by taking the high ground was also important. So, I developed two chants for myself, "Positive thinking brings the advantages I desire," and when my altitude was slipping, "Misery loves company and I'm not going to the pity party." It takes hard work and discipline to maintain a healthy attitude, but it's even harder to fend off people that simply want to bring you down and battle you in the trenches. Years later, first lady Michelle Obama made a great statement, "When they *go low*, we *go* high." When I heard that, I smiled as it reminded me of Jean and his altitude.

When I owned my real estate company, Attitude and Altitude became an important and frequent conversation. We once had about 40 full-time, experienced agents and sometimes they could be a handful and an emotional rollercoaster. One day I hired this young, somewhat inexperienced agent, who I thought with the right training and direction would be a very successful agent. Not only was he young, but he was funny, gregarious, and was eager to be trained and learn as much as he could. He was like a sponge for knowledge and was highly driven to be successful, and honestly, he made me laugh. When he joined our firm, the market was somewhat in the tanks and many of our agents were getting a little negative... no, very negative. I found myself giving pep talks and cheerleading half of my time at the office. The newbie, as some would call him, came to my office and asked if I had a minute to chat. I said yes, and invited him in. We talked about using systems and dialogues to generate more business and marketing ideas for self-promotion. At one point I told him how he was a real asset to our company and I was glad he'd joined our team. He looked at me with a smile, but was confused and said how could he be an asset when there is so much talent and experience here? I said you have a great smile and even better, a great attitude, and it's infectious not only with our agents but with your clients, as it instills confidence and that's what's needed in a challenging market... clients do not want a Debbie Downer working for them.

We had monthly sales meetings in our office and it was difficult to come up with material to maintain proper attendance and bring value to the meetings. Shortly after having my attitude/ Debbie Downer talk with the newbie, let's call him Rich, I asked Rich if he wanted to participate in the next meeting and have some fun? He was eager and proud to be asked and signed on quickly. I developed an agenda around the concept of, "Why would a buyer or seller choose me as their agent?" We would have an open brainstorming talk and write down all the good ideas and concepts to make the case. My secret agenda was to discuss and focus on attitude and altitude, which were getting poor and low in our office. During a break in the action, on a serious and firm note, I asked Rich, what is his blood type? He firmly answered, "A Positive." Then I asked him, what does A positive mean? He answered back, "NEVER B negative," which came with a loud laugh and the clapping of hands by the agents. I then asked him to explain, and he went on to explain our well-orchestrated plan of how a healthy attitude and proper altitude are essential in dealing with people, getting clients, and putting deals together. The message was well-received.

So, what's the point? The point is, your attitude is everything and people want to work with and deal with people that are optimistic and confident. The world loves winners, and honestly, being a winner is somewhat easy just by having a genuine smile, an air of confidence, and the ability to outmaneuver negative people.

AGREE TO AGREE

You will be amazed by the number of people that fear the very thought of being involved with a negotiation, dispute, or some type of mediation process. For most people, negotiation is conflict right from the start. Whether buying a car or negotiating a business deal, it's perceived as tension pure and simple. What follows that perception is anxiety, reluctance, and an automatic defense shield. The problem with all of this is that these folks are somewhat scared and prepare themselves for a fight. They don't want to get beat up, taken advantage of, or involved with some kind of mental gymnastics, so they go into the situation with an attitude that they are entering a hostile environment. That type of thinking is infectious, so the counterpart takes on a similar but opposite approach and the general mood is compromised from the start. To many, the words "negotiations," "dispute resolution" and "mediation" have negative connotations. That does not have to be the case. We simply need to educate these folks that these terms or labels are not about a potential conflict, but instead are a product of good dialog and communication with a goal of a mutually acceptable agreement. It does not need to be complicated. We're here to form an agreement that all parties are satisfied with. The beauty of an agreement is, for the most part, the sky's the limit. Meaning that with a cordial brainstorming session folks can create any type of outcomes regarding terms and conditions when nothing is off the table. Basically, you create a free-thinking zone. It's all about the initial setup and meeting to agree to agree. No need for drama. It's just about achieving goals and results. There is no doubt that there needs to be an adult in the room and might as well be you. It's your job to control the beast and set the tempo. The goal is to start the dialog with respect and ease while avoiding the perception that a negotiation is a sparring match when it's nothing more than a simple agreement between two parties.

I had a commercial vacant lot that I personally owned, but my plans changed and I decided to sell it, so I put it on the market for $1,200.000. I received a call from a commercial broker who was a gentleman that I had worked with in the past. Nice guy, however, from my experience working with commercial brokers, they had a tendency to overcomplicate a deal. But that was coming from someone whose business was mostly residential. He was representing a nonprofit group that was interested in building their headquarters and the location was perfect for them. I shared site plans, utility plans, soil data, and then we met for a site visit. Things were looking good; I had a qualified buyer and a perfect end user. Things changed when their broker called me and wanted to set up a meeting with his buyer's attorney. My first question was, who is he? When he told me who it was, my reaction went from joy to dismay, as I had worked with this guy before and he was brutal. His style was to beat you up with bully techniques and threats. I naturally assumed we would butt heads and end up with no deal. I told the broker to set up the meeting and I prepared myself for a Karate match with punches, kicks, and throws. My price of $1,200,000 was flexible in the beginning, as I would be happy with $1,000,000 for a normal, no-drama deal. But with this guy, I was going to hold out for full price, as I could care less if I sold the property with this guy involved. I walked into the meeting and we made the cordial introductions, but the air was thick. The attorney started off first, and to my surprise, thanked me for the meeting. He said, "I know we've had some differences in the past, but I would like to ask you if we could put the past aside and see if we could put a deal together." He went on to explain how he was representing this nonprofit, as it's a cause that he supports and will be doing at no charge to his client. Dumfounded, I said that's great, I am all ears. He went on to say that the property was perfect for his client, that their top budget is $1,000,000 cash and they would need 30 days for due diligence and could close in 90 days or less. I said to myself, What the hell just happened? No fight. No back and forth. All this mental anguish and preparation for a fight and nothing. I said that that all that sounded fine and that we had a deal. One-minute negotiation. To his credit, the attorney took charge as the alpha dog, changed the narrative, set the expectation for no drama, and put his cards on the table. I was impressed and thankful he came to the table with the attitude to agree to agree.

One of the phrases that I have heard over the years when involved with a negotiation that was at an impasse was, "Well, I guess we agree to disagree." To me, it was like fingernails on a chalkboard. My response was always, "I am sorry, but no, I don't want to disagree, I would prefer that we continue and look for ways we can expand the value of this conversation by looking for concessions and compromises. Let's not walk away with nothing except a bad taste in our mouths." A couple of things, however, that one needs to keep in mind for being the agreeable one. First, you do not want to set yourself up as a pushover by being open, honest, and wanting an agreement. Second is that if at some point your counterpart, for whatever reason, appears they do not want a deal or simply becomes evasive. I have had this happen to me many times when I am working for a yes, and I am constantly getting a no. At some point, when I truly think we have reached a good deal for the both of us, and still get a no, I have to stop and ask my counterpart, has something changed, or have you changed your mind about doing this deal? Their reaction is often the same, they shrug their shoulders, shake their head side to side, and just mumble. I continue, I am serious. If something has changed or you have second thoughts, I will respect that and each of us can move on with no animosity. If you do this, two things are going to happen, either they will give you a sigh of relief and admit they're having second thoughts and no longer want the deal, or the best outcome, they say, no that's not the case, why would you ask that? I sometimes refer to the duck and delay tactic to improve their position. At some point you need to call them out and ask the hard question, do you want to do a deal. Having the strength to stop the no agreement routine and instead ask the simple question do they want to continue the dialog with the sincere thought that you are willing to walk away, may only strengthen your position and accelerate the deal.

So, what's the point? The point is going into a negotiation with a healthy attitude and a non-combative approach. Do your best to concentrate on building trust and rapport with your counterpart first. Make them feel that this is a collective and inclusive approach, where each party has the ability to be open, honest, and understanding. There is no need for grand-standing or browbeating, just an approach where you're both looking for a mutually acceptable agreement. It takes two to tango. Your willingness to be agreeable is not a sign of weakness, but an air of confidence. The word negotiation can be scary for some, but it's your job to remove the anxiety and replace it with an environment of creativity to find a common ground known as an agreement.

BUT... CAN YOU DELIVER

Fortunately for me, early on, I developed a mindset that I would make sure that when I promised folks that I would get back to them, I would get back to them as quickly as I could with an answer, feedback, or I am still working on it. Either way, it was entered on my daily task schedule as an action item to get down and the follow-up needed to be done without emotional or workload delay. I considered follow-up as a path to completion and lack of follow-up as a roadblock. What did take me a while to master was just saying no to something that I was not able to do or because of time restraints, could not commit to. Sure, over time that cost me business, but saved me from a lot of mental time and aggravation for not over committing and executing poor performance. In the long run, I think people respected me enough that I was honest enough to say no, I am not able at this time and they would look for alternatives. I acted on my belief that follow-up, feedback, and fulfillment deliver results.

On the flip side, it drives me crazy when people say that they're going to do something or commit to a task and for whatever reason, with no lack of excuses, they will not follow through and simply fade away from their promise. To be honest, this is a negative mindset, but one based on experience and reality. Over the years, I have to admit that I became cynical and wary of people not doing their job. My office pals even call me a pain in the ass for being a follow-up hound. My cynicism is based on the concept of "once bitten, twice shy" and that I would need to be the bandleader to prompt people along the way to complete a commitment or job. Sad to say, but I automatically assumed that people will get lazy with their follow-through and I would need to be ready for them, to give them a gentle push to keep things going. When things got a little slow with my counterpart, I was never afraid to contact them and ask, where are we at. If you say to someone that you will get back to them, then, by all means, get back to them, even if you don't have an answer for them, simply say, I don't have the answer yet, but I am working on it. When working a deal, the old cliche "no news is good news" is out the door and should be replaced with a follow-up like "no news yet, but I am working on it." To be a great deal maker, your follow-up skills need to be perfected. Follow-up can be answers to key questions, removing obstacles, clarity on broad statements, and valuable feedback to proposed terms and conditions. Follow-up is simple communication with the purpose of continuing active participation to keep the deal alive. Without proper follow-up or feedback, human nature dictates that most people, particularly business people, have little or no patience in waiting for a callback or an answer to an offer or question. Nobody likes the waiting game and when more time rolls on, people tend to get anxious and think for the worst and the silence further complicates the deal.

What is far worse than the poor follow-up is that people for whatever reason will commit to something that they may not be able to deliver. I understand that unforeseen actions could alter one's commitment and timetable; however, if one makes a promise to complete a task or agreement, knowing there is a slim chance of completing it, is outright wrong, destructive, and typically ends in a negative-sum deal.

Our construction company owned a small parcel of land in the central part of Massachusetts and was in an area that would be difficult for our construction crew to manage. It was a 4-acre parcel and perfect for a three-story office condominium complex. We made the decision to hire a general contractor to handle the entire build from start to finish as our crews were straight out busy. The good news was that the overall real estate market was in our favor, so we could absorb the extra costs. We also hired an outside real estate marketing company to handle the sales and marketing efforts on our behalf as well. We figured that our margins would be lower but wanted to take advantage of a vibrant market without using any of our resources, which certainly sounded good on paper. We interviewed several general contractors and narrowed them down to three contractors that we thought would do a great job on the project. We sharpened our negotiation skills and met with all three companies separately and went over all the plans, specifications, and urgency of a completed project. In retrospect, I think we got a little too carried away on pushing hard for price concessions and playing hardball for a low bid. We were all great negotiators, and it was simply instinct and training and that the idea of losing control of the build and marketing kind of spooked us, hence looking to lower costs was important to us. Well, our aggressive approach scared off one of the contractors and now we were left with only two. We asked both companies to get us a full bid in 21 days, which was plenty of time for them. We figured if we gave them plenty of time, they could feel more comfortable giving us their best and accurate bid they could live with. Because we had our own construction company, we knew pretty much what the range of cost to build should be. Well, within

14 days, both contractors submitted their bids. The first contractor came in just about where we thought the build price should be. The second contractor, to our surprise, came 7% under the first contractor's bid and we looked at each other and yelled home run! We called the second contractor and thanked them for the timely bid and told them that their bid was more than fair and was curious how they were able to come in so low. They said that they had lower overhead, access to reasonable sub-contractors, and the timing for the project was perfect for them. We said you have a deal and we immediately contacted the other contractor and thanked them for their prompt bid, but explained to them that we decided to go with another contractor. We signed a contract with the lower bidder and gave them a down payment that would cover the initial site work and foundation. Within weeks, they were doing site work and preparing for the foundation. We were all gloating how we negotiated a killer deal on the build, which set us up for a windfall profit well-above projection. Did someone say bonus! Within the next few weeks, the foundation went in and things were looking pretty good. All of a sudden, nobody is on the job site, no lumber, no materials... nothing. A chill went up to my spine and my first thought was what my gut told me when we received the bid. If it's too good to be true, then it's probably not true. I had a feeling that the bid was too low and how could this company make money without cutting costs and corners. But our overzealous thought of more profits and our hardball negotiation tactics blinded us from the reality that it was a great deal for us and an awful deal for them. The next few weeks were a duck and delay from the contractor. Eventually, we arranged a meeting with them and they basically said that they were about ready to go bankrupt and suppliers would not extend credit and they thought this job would bail them out. They went on a hope and prayer that the suppliers and lenders would stick with them for this job. They were wrong. We

thought about suing them but determined that it would be like getting blood out of a rock and it would be smart to just move on. Fortunately, we paid them only for what they did so we weren't too upside down on the build. But it was now about timing, as we were starting from scratch again. We went to the other contractor with our tail between our legs, but they had accepted another job and were not available. We managed to use our own resources and limp along with construction and with delays and added cost we were lucky to turn a small profit. Did someone say, absolutely no bonus! We learned a giant lesson on that project. You can be the best negotiator out there, but if your counterpart can't deliver on his end of the bargain, you have nothing but a negative-sum deal. Meaning it will cost you more to retool and make up for lost time. It's very important to realize that everybody has to win and implementation of the deal has to be a major topic in the negotiation.

We were lucky to get a small win but at the expense of our counterparts' loss. The reality is we both lost. They lost their business and we chipped away a little of our integrity and reputation. We should have known with our experience with construction costs that this was a horrible deal for the contractor and we missed the opportunity to partner better with them or certainly offer a fairer deal for them with a positive outcome.

So, what's the point? The point is that you can be a super negotiator, but if your counterpart cannot deliver the product or promise, you may wind up with a negative sum deal, which may be worse than if you had no deal at all. Yes, it is your job to negotiate a good deal on you or your client's behalf, but when implementation matters, both sides need a win to survive the deal, otherwise it becomes easy for one to simply walk away from the deal and let the chips fall. Avoid doing a deal that your gut or experience tells you that your counterpart may not be able to fulfill.

Once a deal is made, commit with follow-up and follow-through, with constant, consistent communications knowing both sides need to contribute to achieving a wonderful outcome. Exercise excellence... do what you say, communicate what you mean, and deliver what you promise.

GET REAL

My first real job started when I was in high school. I worked for this local company that made precision aluminum parts for the aerospace industry. I started off doing various random tasks like sweeping the floors and sandblasting parts, which was fine with me as I needed the cash. The company was unique, as five owners had quit their company in California to start a similar one in NH. The unique thing for me was not the job I had to do, but the people for whom I was working. First, they were from California, which for them, coming to NH must have been a culture shock. For me, they were new, different, and interesting. I was excited to be hanging out with people from basically another planet. Second, all five of them had very different personalities and I could learn from each. Living at home for me, was kind of a sad situation, as my mother and father had personal issues/problems. Consequently, role models were absent from my childhood. So, if I was not getting the guidance from home, I figured that I needed to get it from outside the home and therefore I always searched for people that I could look up to, and learn from. Well, working with these folks, I hit a home run. These guys were smart, exciting, and totally accessible, as this was a small start-up business and the owners were hands-on operators. I made it clear that I enjoyed working for them and would do anything they wanted me to do. I did my job as best as I could but studied them like a Hawk. Carl, my favorite, was like a father to me and taught me if I worked hard, played by the rules, I'd always do well. Dan was just an all-around nice guy that always looked happy with his natural smile. Bill was a big man, another happy-go-lucky, that would always stop and ask how I was doing and constantly would ask me what he should have for lunch? He always made me feel special. Zeke was a unique character, who was also smart but seemed to be in his own little world. He was not a people person, but fun to watch and study. Lastly, there was D. Don, Not Don or Dennis, but D. Don. He was the Vice President of sales and marketing, the future image of Paul/Me. This was the person I could learn a lot from, so I watched his every move. This guy was smooth, dressed for success, handsome, and well-groomed. I used to envision myself as him, walking into meetings, taking charge, and putting deals together. If I was anything back then, I was an excellent dreamer. The biggest takeaway from what I learned from D. Don, which would become one of the most influential and important characteristics of my career, was his lack of authenticity. On the surface, he was a polished, charismatic front person, but dig just a little he was just a good-looking fake. I remember when I would pass him walking down the hallway, and I would say good morning, Mr. D. Without acknowledging me, he wouldn't look me in the face, he would pass by and say, "How ya doing?" I watched him interact with the other owners and he was no different to them, just a simple bullshit artist. One time I was hanging around the front office and a couple of the owners were in the conference room next door. I could hear them talking about D. Don. One of the owners said that D. Don was so full of himself, that nobody liked dealing with him and that he was hurting sales. They were trying to figure out what to do, particularly because D. Don was an equal partner. I slowly vanished around the corner and was blown away by the fact that my idol on the surface was nothing more than a flash in the pan, who was doing more harm than good to his own company. His inability to simply be sincere and caring was not possible, or certainly not a trait I wanted, and his lack of authenticity blocked any potential he might have had to connect with people. What a waste, I said to myself, you would think it would be easy and beneficial to go out of your way to make people feel special and treat them like you would like to be treated. I guess not, as I've met a lot of D. Don's in life. Well, it was very interesting for me to learn at an early age that what I could learn from someone was a person I don't want to be. From that point on, I would focus my mental training on making sure that I genuinely cared what people said. I would listen and try to understand what people meant. I would have eye-to-eye, and belly-to-belly sincere conversations, no matter the subject or the person. I wanted to be a people person, by treating everyone the same with respect while speaking from the heart. I think it paid off, as I would eventually enjoy talking to people and became a Curious George by engaging in conversations I never would have engaged in before. If I simply smiled, listened, and asked questions I was amazed how people would open up and tell me things that I thought were really personal and somewhat private. I believe that they were convinced that I was sincere and really cared about what they said. Most of all, I made a point not to judge what they said or thought. The more I asked, the more they answered. Many times, I would keep the conversation going by responding to their comments with "That's a great point", or "I totally understand that" or "I never thought of that" or "That makes sense." I just wanted to reward them with positive feedback for being so forthcoming. In the end, I genuinely wanted to be the real deal, authentic, caring, and create a no-judgment zone.

So, what's the point? The point is that when dealing with people you can be a fake, fast talker, and get little or no information from your counterpart, or you can be a sincere, caring person and get real and accurate information from your counterpart. The choice is simple and easy and it does not make you vulnerable for trying to be a good person instead; it makes you more confident and successful by using a soft approach. I've always been under the understanding that with more information you can make better decisions and, if you're authentic and compassionate in your approach, you will get more information. I always do my absolute best to put myself in the other person's position, look through their eyes, listen through their ears, and do my best to understand what they're thinking, and what they want. I just want to be sure that I fully understand the information that they are giving me and not misinterpret it. I want them to trust me and to create an environment where I can hear and understand the other side of the story. As I always preached, I can deal with the known, but I can't deal with the unknown. Be real, authentic, and learn the ability to connect with people and you will get the truth, their needs, wants, and urgencies.

THE GIFT

There was a time in my early career days in real estate that I was always in competition with some of my colleagues for a position in the top ten sales roster. Our real estate brokerage company was one of the largest in New England and my direct competition was a bunch of young bucks like myself energetically vying for a position on the coveted monthly top ten producer list. The top five were always the same older, established folks that were consistent and successful with their productivity. The remaining spots were an open competition for all, with a combination of luck and hard work. Knowing that sales are simply a contact sport, I would ramp up my calls, work my sphere of influence, and go out and ask for business. Prospecting and business development were always a chore for me to stay focused and consistent, but making the top ten list was my carrot for motivation. Of course, I was not alone. There were about a dozen of us young Lads and Ladies battling for a spot on the list.

There was this one guy, Leo, that always gave me a run for my money. We were about the same age, co-workers, but not friends as such. Leo and I were both members of a local health club and frequented it quite often. I was there for one purpose, exercise, Leo, not so much. I would make my rounds through the weigh stations and eventually would land on the Stairmaster. My attire was simple, shorts and a tee-shirt. While on the Stairmaster, I would often see Leo enter the club. He walked in like a movie star with a velour two-piece matching tracksuit. He looked like George Hamilton with his perpetual tan and his stylish flowing dark hair. He would walk around with his confident smile meeting and greeting people with a soft handshake or a pat on the back. From time to time, he would pick up a set of dumbbells, do a couple of lifts, and then continue on and work the room. He would make me laugh as well as jealous, how he was able to talk to everyone and get them to smile and be open to whatever he was saying. I thought his approach was a little phony, but not to his audience, they loved him. He spoke with sincerity, eye to eye, was always full of compliments, and always talked about them and not himself. How're the kids, how's the family, heard you got a promotion, and so on was his style. His natural ability to connect with people, win their rapport, and build relationships was amazing. His approach worked well and he was rewarded by receiving many real estate referrals from his loyal group of homegrown advocates.

I would see him from time to time in the office and I would always call him Lucky Leo to his face, but behind his back, I would call him Joe Schmooze. Caddy yes, but I did have a genuine admiration of him. Yes, I called him Lucky Leo, but the more I got to know him, I discovered it was not luck for his success, but a gift. He was born with the gift of Gab, which is a natural way of speaking easily and openly with people, building trust, influencing outcomes, and persuading decision-making. Leo nailed it and became a frequent name on the monthly top ten wall of fame.

Around the same time and in the same area, I had a friend, Pedro, who was an account representative for a large family-owned service industry business. He was one of the sons of the owners and naturally had a little more pressure to succeed which he did masterfully. He did not have the Leo look, but quite the opposite, more like the traditional New England look with his button-down, triple starched white shirt, stylish eyeglasses, and a haircut from the corner barber. He did not like to be considered a salesperson because he felt as though it was a tiny piece of what he offered. Yes, he had to sell his service, negotiate the terms, deliver the goods, monitor quality control, but most of all, maintain a great lasting relationship with his clients. But like Leo, he was the ultimate schmoozer. Leo, although very successful in his approach, was not my style, but Pedro was a bona fide Joe Smooth.

Pedro had a master's in the gift of gab and took the art of schmoozing to a greater level. He was authentic in his approach and his goal was to make everyone he spoke with feel like they were someone special. His genuine sense of humor and constant compliments made everyone he touched smile. He would do background research on everyone he needed to deal with in order to find out if they were married, had kids, favorite things, sports, hobbies, anything to be able to better connect with them. He would send them gifts, note cards, and stop by their place of business to simply say hi. He would never talk about himself unless asked and professed that his client relationship comes first before any talk about business. At times, there was so much talk about personal niceties, that there was hardly any time to talk about business. But who cared, they were all happy, loved him, and trusted his service. His human approach was so successful, that there was little need to sell, just to follow-up on referrals from his happy client base. His relationships were so strong that negotiation efforts were basically a simple chat and a rubber stamp. He also had the gift, and I watched his approach with inquisitiveness and admiration.

At that time, I did not have that natural gift of gab. I was a little too serious, wound a little too tight, and did not possess the natural ease in dealing with people. I had to work longer and harder to get lesser results as Leo and Pedro would achieve. I had convinced myself that schmoozing was fake and gabbing meant I would talk too much. But as I watched Leo and Pedro, they were having fun with what they were doing, they created a business fan club, and their sales productivity was through the roof. Envious of their sales performance, I quickly surrendered to the fact that they were right and I was wrong and it was time for a new approach in dealing with people. I studied their approach and delivery system and although I did not have their natural gift, I was convinced with training and practice I could acquire or replicate their style. I was still hung up on the label schmooze, so I decided to rename it as charm. The word charm seemed to be more professional and businesslike to me and with that, I committed to myself to strive to be more charming in dealing with people. I mentally enrolled in the Pedro-Leo charm school and wrote down all their attributes for their gift, schmooze, and charm. The following characteristics are what I believed summarized their pathway to connect and build close, harmonious relationships with people.

1. Speak with a gentle smile.
2. Maintain eye contact when you speak.
3. Listen with undivided interest.
4. Relax and speak slowly.
5. Always remember their name.
6. Never talk about yourself unless asked.
7. Maintain a sense of humor.
8. Get people to laugh and lighten up.
9. Show genuine interest in them.
10. Make fun of yourself.

11. Apologize for your mistakes.
12. Engage in small talk and silly stories.
13. Never criticize or complain.
14. Praise and compliment.
15. Recognize, acknowledge, and appreciate.
16. Be honest and sincere.
17. Give thanks, show gratitude.
18. Never look to win a conversation.
19. Share positivity.
20. Follow-up with personal note cards, phone calls, and visits.
21. Show empathy, be nice.
22. Maintain common ground and stay informal.
23. Make them feel special.

Not knowing how this new approach would work for me, I decided to practice it on non-business folks. I called my local cable company to see if I could lower my bill. Charmed the hotel reservation person for a free upgraded room. Schmoozed the restaurant hostess for a better table. Connected with a car salesman to get a better deal. One of my more challenging charm endeavors was convincing the ticket taker to allow me to enter a sold-out concert with no ticket (I lost mine). I said to myself, this really works, just be nice, fun, and focus on them and I will get better results. From then on, I would always say people first, then the product or the problem.

So, what's the point? The point is that you need to invest time in people and develop valuable people skills. You need to win people over and with that, they will help you achieve what you're looking for or simply be easier to deal with. There is no shortage of nasty, angry people out there and your counterpart would find it refreshing in dealing with someone nice.

Make their day, make them feel special, and you win a friend and they will help and want you to succeed. As Abraham Lincoln said, "A drop of honey catches more flies than a gallon of gall."

CURIOUS GEORGE

Growing up, my mother always called me Curious George. Apparently, I asked a lot of questions and to some, that can be very annoying, hence the name-calling. I have to admit, I did ask a lot of questions as I was interested in so many things and found people interesting. I don't think I was nosey or obnoxious. I just enjoyed learning from people rather than a book and considered it a free home-grown education. When I reached middle school, quite the opposite happened when I was in an environment where I was supposed to learn. Unfortunately, I was too shy or fearful to ask questions, which honestly bothered me. I was the youngest and smallest boy in the class and I simply was scared of asking potentially stupid questions and having all the kids laugh or snarl at me. The sad truth was that there were many in my class that felt the same way and I think it affected our learning progress. I remember getting so excited when someone in my class had the courage to ask the same question I had, and received a respectable answer. I soon exited that phobia and eventually returned to my Curious George status of asking questions. Not only did I get over what people thought when I asked a question, but I also encouraged others not to be shy about asking questions as well. In my early stage of marketing real estate, I started working for a developer that was only a couple of years older than me.

I think he had the same fear of asking questions as I had back in school. He liked asking a lot of questions, but he had a different twist: he would start from the beginning and say, "Let me ask you a stupid question." He made me laugh, because not once or twice did he say it, but before every question. I kind of liked that approach for a while and used it myself.

As my career started to mature, I quickly dropped the stupid question line but kept the Curious George mindset. I was simply interested in people and what motivates them; How they grew up; What their hobbies were, and on and on. I just found most people fascinating and I was never jealous or envious of people with wealth and who were successful, only curious about how they achieved it. I remember one particular time when I was a young sales manager for a luxury condo development in a rural town on the Massachusetts, New Hampshire border. Nearby in Massachusetts there were a couple of high-end towns and folks would stop by because of the fact we were offering luxury condos with basically no maintenance, so it was attractive to some that were busy or wanted to travel. One day a gentleman drove in with an older four-door Oldsmobile and got out to meet me. He was well-groomed, had a white shirt with jeans, maybe in his fifties, and was just a nice guy. I introduced myself and started talking about the development. Then Curious George kicked in. I asked him if he lived around here? He told me the town where he lived, and to myself, I thought it was great, a nearby high-end town in Massachusetts... yeah. I continued with the tour of the development, then asked, "Do you work around here." He simply said yes. Rats, not enough information. He asked a number of questions, which I answered. Then I asked him what he did for a living? He said he was in the restaurant business. Let's put George on pause for a second, for there was a method to my curiosity. I was trying to determine his motivation, any urgencies, and if he had the financial ability to purchase a home in the community. Continuing with the tour I offered, I'm a foodie. What kind of restaurant do you own? He said he had a hamburger joint. That threw me off, but I continued on like a professional and slid into what's your restaurant? He said he owned a few McDonald's. I said a few? "Yeah, about 40," he said. I gave him a big smile and said that is awesome, good for you. To this day, I don't remember if I sold him a unit, but I was impressed with him and his story.

I developed a natural approach to asking innocent questions to complete strangers not in intrusive ways, but in ways that folks understood I was genuinely interested in. I found that if I asked innocent questions, with no ulterior motives, most times I would get honest answers. In sales and negotiations, this was a clear benefit for my business. I have always said, the more information I have, the better the decision I will make. In dealing with people, the more information you have about them, the better you will understand their needs, wants, and urgencies. I figured the better I got to know them in a non-combative way, the quicker I could build a rapport with them, and the easier it would be to deal with them. If I took the time to build a relationship, I could figure out their likes and dislikes and do my best to not only get what I want but what they wanted as well. The more I knew about them, the better I could figure out how to add value to the deal.

George also has a habit of digging deep. Well before I would meet someone that I was going to be negotiating with, I would research them as best I could. I would Google them, find where they lived, where they worked, if they had a family, any hobbies, or other information I could gather on them to prepare me for who I was going to be dealing with. I know this may make me sound like a stalker of some sort, but I'm not. I guess you could call it opposition research, but I don't think of it that way because I don't want to enter into a negotiation or deal scenario with an attitude that it's me against them. Personally, I want to jump into a situation where I can build trust and relationships early on to achieve a mutually acceptable outcome in the shortest period of time.

So, what's the point? The point is that there is a huge benefit for being a good listener, but of equal importance is knowing the art of asking questions. Asking innocent questions shows interest, which grows respect, which translates into trust. The questions you ask can be sensitive, so you will need to learn to take the mental temperatures of your counterparts and tread lightly early on. Good questions sow honest answers, which gives you better information with which to navigate your needs as well as theirs. Never be shy about asking legitimate questions; in the end, it's good for everyone.

PATIENCE YOUNG GRASSHOPPER

As I mentioned early on in this book, I was a student of martial arts in my twenties. One of my favorite shows on TV was the 1970's series *Kung Fu*. It was about a young martial arts student and his master teaching the art of self-defense. Early on in the show, Master Po becomes a little annoyed with student Chang and named him Grasshopper. Young Grasshopper was becoming quite ignorant to the master's ways and at one point Master Po asked Chang to close his eyes and listen to what he could hear and feel. Chang could hear birds chirping, water flowing, the sound of a grasshopper at his feet, and could sense master Po slowly walking around him. The point Master Po was making to the newly appointed Grasshopper was that patience and silence can determine one's own presence and others' positions. When my personal Karate instructor taught me the value of watching my opponent's eyes that may give away their next move, I would reflect on Master Po's instruction to be patient and study my opponent. It was master Po's teaching that emphasized patience as the ultimate martial arts skill. Going forward with my martial art studies as well as further business dealings, I embraced the concept that a good offense is a well-calculated defense.

It's been said that patience is a virtue and that it is. For most people, including myself, patience is hard work, requires practice, tolerance, and deep breathing, yet it is a very valuable and necessary skill. Typically, business people tend to fall in the Type A category, and for the most part that includes impatience and the tendency to get angry or upset when events don't go their way or take too long. I loved watching people that are naturally patient, quiet, and relaxed right from the get-go. No practice, no deep breathing, just natural. I once worked with a gentleman who fit that description. On one hand, I was jealous that he was so relaxed and laid back all the time, but on the other hand, curiously, I could never figure out what he was thinking. I always said to myself, that man is a walking Valium. On the flip side, there never seems to be a shortage of inpatient players at the deal-making table and they tend to create chaos and tensions to the problem or the product being negotiated. No practice just comes naturally. I learned over time that when I get involved in a dispute or a negotiation that had an aggressive player at the table, I would do my best to slow down the pace and chip away at the apparent roadblocks. I would focus on two roadblocks. First, the mental roadblock that comes with an emotional component, then the physical roadblock which typically is the nuts and bolts of the deal. The emotional component is trying to defuse the aggressive player which requires time and patience. I would listen to them patiently and politely and would allow them to vent and express their ideas, thoughts, and positions. Then I would ask them sincere whys on how they determined that position and can they be flexible. By downshifting the pace, it allows you to take some extra time to ask questions and listen for honest answers. In some cases, time can heal wounds and fix problems. I want to be patient and take the time to really figure out what they're thinking. With that information, I can move on to the physical component and focus on the nuts and bolts.

In dealing with people, I want to get to the truth as to what they need and want. It's not necessarily what they're saying but what they are thinking, and figuring out what they are really thinking may take time and patience. I don't want to hurry the situation, thinking I would get faster results; I want to do my best to take the time to get my desired results. I have said before, I can deal with the known, but I can't deal with the unknown. Simply put, you don't want to force a deadline which may cause a dead-end.

Patience can also be a unique tool in your negotiation arsenal. When the issue at hand is getting out of control and you have an aggressive counterpart with unreal demands, sometimes I use patience to slow the pace and go silent. I let them do all the talking and when they run out of steam, they look for you or someone else to carry the conversation. When no one takes the bait, they continue to ramble. Their personalities do not process quiet, so if the table goes quiet, they continue the chitchat. It is quite amusing to watch your counterpart dig for words or scratch for ideas that will hopefully reengage the folks at the table. If the silent treatment continues, Mr. Aggressive will enter his mental gymnastics stage and start to worry if his audience has lost interest or worse, willing to step away from the table without a deal. He wrestles mentally with what people are thinking and what they are willing to do. Fear of loss is a great motivator and without any substance from his counterpart, he starts to worry. This uneasy feeling, combined with mental fatigue, creates a new environment where he is poised for a position change and may back off his initial demands. This is when the smart negotiator jumps back in and looks for alternatives to his demands and seeks a more equitable deal for all parties. This technique is tricky, as you may be risking a deal, but if you don't have an acceptable deal on the table already, it's worth the gamble.

FAILED TO NEGOTIATE THE DEAL

When I was working for an international construction company, one of my jobs was land acquisitions. We had the construction infrastructure to build large residential and commercial developments. We always had to have potential developments lined up to keep our building machine operating consistently. I was part of a division that had two full-blown construction companies under us and keeping them busy was always a challenge. Early on in my employment, sadly, the President of our group passed away and they never replaced him. I must say it was kind of weird not having a boss in the United States, but I did my job responsibly and they trusted me. My new boss was one of the managing directors of the parent company in the UK and he was Welch with a very distinct accent. We were running low on land acquisitions, and I happened to find a perfect piece of land off of a major highway that was a no-brainer for a mixed-use residential and office condo development. The broker handling the property was a friend of a friend and I was told he was reasonable to deal with. The property was expensive, but with the right number of units, we figured we could make it work. I ran the proposal by my boss in the UK and he said go for it. I knew that the property would have several potential buyers, so I wanted to submit a strong offer quickly. I already had a decent rapport with the broker gaining information about the property, so I felt comfortable dealing with him. We were in a great financial position, so we offered a full-price, cash deal, subject to a reasonable due diligence period. I submitted the offer to the listing broker and when he reviewed it, he gave me a gentle smile and I interpreted that to be a yes. He said that looks good and I will submit it to my seller and get back to you. Perfect, I said, look forward to hearing back from you. Hours later, in my car, I am tooling down route 95 in Massachusetts, and my car phone rings. This was in a time when cell phones were basically bag phones and not very reliable and very expensive. I picked up the phone to a hissing noise and it was my boss in the UK. Hello, Paul, he said, with a severe echo. His accent was brutal and my name to him was not Paul but Poole, as in swimming pool. With the hissing, echo, and accent, he asks me if I put the land deal together. I said no, I just submitted it a few hours ago. He goes on to tell me that this deal is important to keep the train going, make it happen. I said I understand, I am on it. I did not hear from the broker that evening, so in the morning I called him up for an update. He had not received a response from the seller yet, kind of unusual, he added and by the way, I did receive two more offers. Good for you and bad for me, I said. Back in my car and my phone rings and I get the hissing, echo, and hello, Poole, did you put the deal together? Not yet, the seller has not responded back to his broker yet. Stay on top of this, don't let it slip through the cracks, we need this deal, he barked back. Do you think we should increase our offer, he asked? No, I know what I am doing and I am not going to negotiate with myself, let's be patient. I shook my head and carried on. I called the listing broker back in the evening and apologized for the late call but was looking for an update. He said he still has not heard back from the seller and went on to thank me for being patient. He continued saying that the other two buyers' agents were all over him and accused him of shopping the deal and were rude and disrespectful. I fully understand, I have a boss that's always on edge...he laughed. I reiterated our deal was full price, cash deal, and no drama and if his seller would like to meet or need anything from us, please feel free to ask. The next day, like clockwork, my phone rings, I get the hiss, echo, and Poole have you put the deal together yet. No sir, for whatever reason the seller has gone silent and the listing broker still has not heard from the seller. What is wrong with these people, we give them a clean, cash deal and they can't get back to us he screams. Relax, I am on this, I have a good rapport with the broker and I am sure I will get this done. As soon as I told my boss across the pond to relax, I knew that was a mistake. Relax is not what I do, he barked, and I don't pay you to relax as well. Stop being nice and put the deal together. I don't remember if I said this or dreamed it up well before Verizon, but I ended by saying you're breaking up, can you hear me, and hung up. Visibly shaken but not stirred, I continued on my drive and the phone rang again. No hissing, no echo, just a hey, Paul, good news, we have a deal. Wow, that's awesome, what happened? He said his seller finally called him back and apologized for the delay, but he had a serious medical scare that took priority. I went over the offers with him and explained that the other agents were jerks to deal with and you were a gentleman, patient, and had a strong deal, so he said to sign her up. I called my boss and told him we got the deal. He said, nice job, Poole, I knew you could do it.

So, what's the point, Poole? The point is there is value in being patient. For most of us, patience is not a natural skill but an acquired skill and one that takes a lot of discipline and practice. In my world, there are two sides to being patent. One is the ability to hit the pause button and mentally review what is happening or what is not happening when you are not getting your desired results. You have to slow the conversation and ask yourself if you have done all you can do to keep the momentum of the deal. You need to review RAPPARS POINT and feel comfortable that you have asked valuable questions and received honest answers, yet no commitments. This is a point when you need to respect and understand that some people need more time to process information than others. This ability to accept and allow indecision without getting angry or upset will ultimately help your counterpart slowly re-enter the deal-making zone at their own pace. The second side of patience is when the deal is stalled and you're dealing with an aggressive party and you simply go silent like you have lost interest. You simply smile and nod your head, no questions, short answers, and let them keep the conversation going; my mother was a master at this. Your counterpart will start to wonder if the deal is over, you're willing to walk away, but ultimately, they will have no clue what you're thinking. As I have said many times, fear of loss is the great motivator and when the sensation of losing the deal and walking away with nothing sends you a little chill sensation, it's like an alarm that a new approach is necessary to win your counterpart back to the table and stop the silent treatment. It's quite simple, when the conversation gets uncomfortable, it may be time to stop, smile, and smell the deal and skip the roses.

CALLING DOCTOR YANG

In the late eighties, I had what I called "a dream job." I was regional Vice President of Marketing for an international construction company based in the United Kingdom. They gave me an amazing compensation package with bonus incentives for performance, and a gorgeous company car, and they left me free to make all the marketing decisions on my own. We had two full-blown construction companies in New England, one in New Hampshire and the other in Massachusetts. I loved my job as they would allow me to be creative with an open checkbook and they trusted me. Fast forward to 1991, the real estate market in the U.S. was in the tank. With no warning, corporate out of London sent us a dispatch saying that they were shutting down all operations in New England and laying off everyone except me and the VP of Finance. I was shocked but not surprised, given the state of the economy. Eventually, they offered me a position down south with one of their other businesses, but I declined as I did not want to leave New Hampshire. Fortunately, I negotiated an employment contract with a generous severance package in the event that they shut down or relocated for any reason, so financially, I was in good shape. Out of a job and in a horrible real estate market, I was back to square one. I made a decision to move from southern New Hampshire to the Seacoast of New Hampshire and start from scratch.

Once settled, I tried to figure out what to do moving forward. I finally decided on opening a real estate office in Portsmouth NH in the summer of 1992. I bought a RE/MAX franchise and off I went. I had the finances to build out a nice office and hire great staff. Next, I was in the agent recruiting business, which was a chore, but I got good at it. I was extremely well versed in negotiations, contract law, finance, appraisals, and the general knowledge of running a successful real estate office. We were growing fast and my management style was an open-door policy. All was going well until I was consumed by the agents with the "got a minute" syndrome. Mentally, I defined a minute as 60 seconds, but in this case, it could be hours. The agents would stroll by my office and wait for an opening and ask if I have a minute. The answer was always yes, of course. The problem was that most of their issues had nothing to do with real estate. There were family issues, money problems, pets, and spouse problems, you name it, I heard it. I became a good listener, but better yet, a great psychiatrist. I somehow morphed from a real estate broker to a shrink. I thought about smoking a pipe, donning a bow tie, adding a couch to my office, and starting off all conversations with how is your day going. I was amazed at how successful these folks were, however, how emotional they could get and how it affected their sales and negotiation performance. Sadly, they were not alone. I had succumbed to the stress and long hours of the business and was developing negative emotions myself that were clearly affecting my performance.

It finally hit home when one of our top producers, who was a high-maintenance, ankle-biting person, was getting on my nerves. Their assistant called me one day and demanded that I take care of a bad deal that they created. I snapped back and said, why is it my job to clean up all of your messes? Right off, I knew that response was a highly emotional mistake. Of course, this type of response got quickly back to the agent. Naturally, there was no shortage of real estate companies out there trying to hire this agent and sure enough, they immediately gave me notice that they were leaving for another company. Because I could not control my emotions, I let 25 million dollars of real estate productivity go out the door. Insult to injury, they convinced another agent to go with them as well, adding up to 40 million losses for my mental bad behavior. To this day I am still pissed that I allowed my emotions to take control over my objectivity. I learned a very painful lesson that day. To be an effective manager, negotiator, mediator, or salesperson you must take into consideration not only the physical, tangible part of the deal or problem but most important and foremost, the emotional state of all the parties involved. Going forward for me, I trained myself to perform a mental health check before I got into any important negotiations or serious conversations. I made sure I was fine and if so, would work on my counterpart next before any talk about a product or problem. I wanted us all emotionally free. I eventually became an admirer of the Chinese philosophy of Yin and Yang. Where there is a negative and positive that can be complementary and interconnected and balance emotions and rationale. I considered Yin to be the negative, dark side and Yang to be the positive, bright side. So, if I went into a situation that was emotionally charged, I would put on my fictitious hat as Doctor Yang. I would do my best to alleviate any tensions or stress and turn to positive thoughts and mutual understandings before any serious conversations regarding negotiations.

Being in the real estate business, I worked with a lot of contractors. There was this one guy who was a painting contractor that I worked with quite a lot. He was a young, quick wit, a street-smart guy that was full of energy and made me laugh. He did a lot of paintwork on houses that were our clients or are own investments. While on the job he consistently listened to talk radio nonstop and knew everything about everything, or at least he had an opinion on everything. My nickname for him was simply the Professor. From time to time, we would talk about business and one time our topic was negotiations and dealing with people. The Professor, as he enjoyed being called, said to me that negotiations and dealing with people should be quite easy if done correctly. How so, I said. He went on to say that those dealings are similar to house painting. He said dealing with people is like applying paint and with the proper preparation, should go well. The challenge is not the painting, but the condition of the house, and in your case, the people that you're dealing with. He went on to say, "I walk into a house, and rarely do I feel that the home is ready for painting. I see cracks in the walls, holes that need to be filled, deal with some flaking, and take care of rough edges and plenty of uneven surfaces. Only after proper attention to those details, do I start to paint." He went on to say that the wise negotiator would do a similar procedure. Never start a negotiation without sensing the mental and emotional state of the people involved. Are they sick, tired, stressed, happy, or sad? Try to address their issues and concerns upfront. Get them to relax, vent, and listen and get them to think and talk through any anxieties or distress. Get the folks that you're dealing with in a comfort zone and only then go on to serious business. I thanked the Professor for his Thesis and acknowledged that his comparison made a lot of sense. He was spot on, as a lot of us tend to jump right into a negotiation without any regard for one's physical or emotional health.

Throughout this book, I mention people first then the product or problem. What do I mean by that? In dealing with any negotiation, dispute, or physical exchange, I want to concentrate on the people involved and their emotional/mental state first, including my own as a priority. I personally need to be mentally fit before the start of any serious dialogue with others, free of any anger, anxiety, or stress. Psychologists would call this

Emotional Intelligence. This is a skill that needs to be acquired to be able to emotionally manage yourself and, of equal importance, be able to communicate effectively and have the ability to defuse conflict. This essential skill requires you to be a great listener, understand one's needs, and be an effective relationship manager. Once you feel that you are in the correct mindset, or fully centered, then can you move on to your counterpart's emotional state. You start with respect for the folks at the table, build a relationship, forge a rapport and earn trust. The goal is to create an environment where your counterpart can vent anger, express concerns, and confide in you about their own personal problems. You want to create a space where ideas can flow freely, be optimistic, and be able to smile and laugh. Once all involved sense calm and confidence, then can you move on to the business at hand.

So, what's the point? The point is that emotions play a very important role in dealing with people. Embrace the fact that nearly all negotiations, disputes, and transactions will have an emotional component to them. Your job is to be the emotional manager, starting with yourself, to be able to think clearly, objectively, even-keeled, and calmly. Give time and space to release and restrain negative feelings, while highlighting the positive. Understand that the emotional rollercoaster, if not managed correctly, will go off rail and have negative effects and influences on performance and outcomes.

Listen to them vent, show empathy toward their needs, understand what they want, laugh and giggle, and make negotiations a joyful playground.

THE OBSERVER

While studying martial arts in my younger years, I discovered early on a technique that would help me with negotiating and provide me with a better picture in dealing with people. Each class was a regular routine. We would start off with stretching, practice our kicks and blocks, learn new techniques, and learn and practice Kata's, a series of detailed, fluent moves. At the end of the class, we would spar with each other and have a 3-point match, judged by the instructor for technique and accuracy. Sometimes sparring was optional and sometimes not, but my hand was always up, as I was there to learn and excel. The quickest way to learn was to spar often, take the punishment, and learn from my mistakes. My instructor liked my attitude and was always giving me special tips on how to deal with my opponent. He would tell me, watch their eyes, they will tell you the story for their next move. I took his advice and when I was sparring, I concentrated on my opponent's eyes. Sure enough, whenever they were about to initiate a kick or punch, their eyes would get bigger, then brows would go up or simply flinch just before they started their move. All I needed to figure out was if they were going to throw me a kick or a punch, which I could judge by their stance or set-up. Once they tipped me off by their initiation, I had two choices for a counter move: The first choice was to step back and get out of harm's way; the second and preferred was to jump to them sideways to choke them up and give them a swift and accurate back fist. The second move was always the risky choice, but it always got me a point in the match. It's been said, keep your eyes on the ball, but in martial arts, it's to keep your eyes on your opponent.

We have talked about the importance of asking key questions, listening with care and compassion, but sometimes we get sidetracked by the fact that some people just don't talk. There are a number of reasons for this. Maybe they're shy, maybe they're scared, maybe it's in their DNA to be quiet, maybe they're pissed off, or maybe it's a defense strategy to keep you off guard. Whatever the reason, it is difficult to deal with people that aren't talkers. Early on, for me, it was a challenge, as I was a chronic talker, and had a unique ability to get people talking. Dealing with these non-talking folks was tough, even tougher when there was a group of non-talkers and I felt like I was dealing with myself, which was kind of awkward. So, I figured out an approach where I would start off with simple questions and listen to their response if any, but more importantly I'd watch their response. These quiet folks were pretty good at body language and all I had to do was to translate what their physical response would be by their shrugs, smiles, frowns, rolling eyes, hand movements, and on and on. People can be shy with their words, yet loud with their body movements. Basically, it was a crash course in non-verbal communications 101.

If I was involved with a negotiation or dispute resolution and knew that I would have a room full of non-talkers, I would go in with a colleague. I would prepare a list of questions that my colleague would ask. After each question, I would listen to the response and watch everybody's physical response. As I have said, I can deal with the known, but I can't deal with the unknown and without being too intrusive, my goal was to try to figure out what they wanted and needed. I needed more information to better craft a deal and if it's not by their words, it's by their physical responses and voice tones. I needed to stay heavily engaged in the surroundings and look for hints that would tip me off as to what their hot buttons were. I did my best not to misjudge them or fall into a trap where I made an assumption that was wrong. People watching is what it's called and I actually enjoy it. If you want to get a quick education on human behavior without going to some fancy school, turn on your TV and watch shows without the volume on. It's a good education on how people respond to their body language. It's a telling story.

One time we were involved in a construction dispute with a gentleman that quickly spiraled out of control. He and his attorneys were very aggressive from the start. The difficult issue for us was that we were not at fault or hadn't caused any harm. I guess that was easy for me to say, but in my mind it was true. My policy was that if we had screwed up, the best way to deal with it was to admit the error and then do our best to quickly resolve the problem as delicately as we could. Meaning, stop the bleeding as quickly as we could and move on. I was convinced that we were not at fault but this gentleman would not let it go and his legal team pursued a lawsuit. Unfortunately, our legal system allows anyone to sue anyone for little or no cause and without recourse if, in the end, they are wrong. Hence, I am a big fan of tort reform. We did our best to explain our side of the story, but they were not having it and asked for a large cash settlement. The gentleman was from out of state and may have had a different way of doing business than we did, but my thought was, this was an old fashioned shakedown for cash and I was not going to give in. We tried the usual niceties, but nothing worked, as he said, "I want to play this out." First, we went to mediation and as we explained to the mediator our case,

I watched his response and actions, and he gave me the message; they have no case. I decided to offer the plaintiff an olive branch. I said to the mediator that I would give $5,000.00 to the plaintiff's charity of choice to end this. The mediator said that was very generous, which reinforced my view that there was no case. I figured it was going to cost us a lot more than $5,000.00 in legal fees, so it would be nice for something to go to a good cause. The plaintiff rejected the offer. He wanted to play it out. Months went by, the legal fees climbed higher, and we finally got our day in court. Once we were in court, my participation was somewhat over and it was in the hands of the Judge and the attorneys. I was just going to sit, watch, and observe what was taking place. It was like watching a tennis match. My head would go from left to right and right to left. I watched the plaintiff and he had this sourpuss look on his face and was dressed like an unmade bed. I would watch and listen while the attorneys bantered back and forth, then I would scan the courtroom to watch for more information. I watched the stenographer roll her eyes a few times as the plaintiff's attorney spoke. The security officer was even displaying displeasure with the attorney as he spoke, his forehead, like a billboard, was saying "bull-shitter." The best part, I watched the Judge fidget and get an angry look on his face. I could tell that he was getting annoyed with this attorney and his case. Then out of nowhere, the Judge told their attorney, "That he was looking at everything he said with a jaundiced eye." He looked pissed. Jaundiced eye, I said to myself, what the hell is that, I'd never heard that phrase before. So, I searched it on my phone and read with a smile, how it meant in a cynical and negative way, that we were being tricked. The security guard's mental message to me had been correct, the attorney was a bullshitter. I scanned the courtroom once again and determined that everyone who was watching showed displeasure with this attorney and his case. Even the attorney himself had a desperate look on his face.

At that point, I took out a piece of paper and wrote a note to our attorney. I asked our attorney to ask the judge for a motion to dismiss, as this case is not about facts, it's all about fiction and the plaintiff and his attorneys are abusing the court and its honor. My attorney approached the bench and told the Judge what I wrote and the Judge paused for 15 seconds then said motion to dismiss granted and slammed his gavel down. Case closed. By watching all the people involved and seeing their reactions, I made the decision to take advantage of that moment of discontent and it worked.

So, what's the point? It's been said that words speak louder than actions, but when there is not an abundance of words, or even worse, the words are not believable, then watching the physical reactions can tell a more compelling story. Learn the benefits of simply being quiet, and scanning the people involved, and seeing if you can gather more physical information. Listening to people is always important; however, watching how they deliver their words while watching how others who are also involved with the situation react to those words, are vital for intelligence gathering. To better understand another's position, it's not only what they're saying that's important, but I want to know what they're thinking, for therein lies the truth. It's the truth that I want to deal with, not the speculation.

WAR AND PEACE

I would be remiss and one could be considered naive not to discuss the reality of a hostile conflict or simply put, a war on words. When dealing with people, products, or problems, it's inevitable that at some point you will be involved in a heated exchange or nasty conflict and it would be wise to understand it and be prepared. Taking the turn down hostility road is an ugly, bumpy road and if you navigate correctly, it could turn back to a smooth highway to your destination or a desirable outcome, if not, result in a dead-end disaster. The fuel for such a heated disagreement is out-of-control emotions, fixed positions, tempers, bullies at the table, or simple misunderstandings. Being human, it's to be understood that tension and conflict could rise quickly for the reasons just stated; however, also people tend to act differently when under pressure, emotional strain, and simply just not feeling good. The smart dealmaker will need the mental radar that something is up with their counterpart and focus on their distress first, before they can address the product or problem they're dealing with. People first, I recommended, is the start of relationship building with the goal of trying to figure out and understand your counterpart as to why they are acting with anger and hostility. Do your best to avoid a verbal conflict. Easy said but harder to do is the reality and once engaged, anger management must immediately come to play. Somebody has to be the adult in the room and if you stay focused on your end game, meaning your desired outcome, you should be the adult in the room and take the incoming hits and do your best to diffuse the situation. Your role should quickly change from negotiator to councilor and become their psychologist. Let them rant and rave and listen and understand not only what they're saying, but sense what they're feeling and look to slow the tempo and look for calm. Position yourself not as an adversary or an opponent, but strive to be a friend and confidant to gain and build trust and rapport to figure out what is really bothering them. Once you get a sense of their personal grievances, only then can you be sympathetic toward their needs, whether emotionally or physically. In this situation, I compare this process to a pressure cooker: it will blow off steam and with the right temperature control, create something good.

Early on in my career, I was project manager for a number of condominium projects in New England with a large real estate brokerage firm. My responsibilities were floor plan evaluation, developing features and options, pricing, marketing, and sales. The most important one of course was sales. We took on and I was assigned to a development in southern NH that was going to be 150 units with a mix of townhomes and garden-style condominiums. Being only 150 units, I was the only person that was needed for the onsite sales. The real estate market at the time was in rough shape and interest rates were high, so I had my job cut out for me. Fortunately, we were in a good location and our product was well designed. The builder/developer was a young guy who had a unique style and was known for being a little temperamental. Construction and marketing started and now it is up to me to make sales. No doubt, I was having a rough start and the builder was getting a little anxious and concerned about the lack of traction regarding sales. He would frequent the sales center and interrogate me why we weren't making any sales. I explained that the market was soft and interest rates were high and we needed a few sales under our belt to get some momentum. He would ask me if our product needed changes and I said no, the product was just fine. Then it's your marketing program that is failing us. I defended our marketing efforts and explained everything we were doing to promote traffic to our site, but he continued to become agitated and belligerent. After a few visits from him, I was getting a little cranky with his behavior. Once again, he stormed into the sales center and asked if we had any deals in the works. Not yet I said. He then shouts what's the problem? The price I said. Then he goes ballistic and shouts back that we were the ones that suggested the price. I said yes, an average price for the development that started off low and eventually went higher as we develop momentum in sales. But you rejected that and wanted to start high and look for higher profits. Our position was to pay the pioneer, meaning give the first buyers a break in pricing and get some sales and sold signs out there to create a little urgency or momentum. You have resisted that strategy and it accomplished zero results I said. From there, the conversation went south and he went on to lecture me about his land cost, construction cost, overhead and expected profit. I said all well and fine, but the cost does not equal value and you need to start low and raise prices when we have at least six sales under our belt. Like a firecracker, he exploded and harsh words flowed back and forth uncontrollably. Naturally, I felt guilty as I let this get out of hand and only added to the argument. I tried to slow the pace, lower the volume but to no avail, the damage was already done. Then there was a pause in the action. He looked at me and said you're not the right person for this project and said he will have me replaced. Ouch, I am fired. I said "good luck." As I walked away, embarrassed by my actions, I stopped and turned around to the builder and said it's too bad. I like the project, enjoyed working with you, and if you should change your mind about working with someone that is honest to you, then by all means please give me a call. At the time I was young and cocky. Fortunately for me, I had enough brains to pay him a compliment and keep the door open on my way out. Two days later he called me, apologized, and hired me back. We changed the pricing strategy, increased collaboration between us, and went on to be a profitable, successful project. Not only did we become close friends, but we also went on and did several projects together and he was instrumental in getting me an officer position with a multi-billion-dollar international construction company. A little war ended in peace, friendship, and respect.

Unfortunately, at some time or many times, you will fall victim to a conflict, whether you're the cause or someone else is the cause; the reality is that war happens. The best thing you can do is understand that arguments will happen and you need to be prepared and trained on how to deal with them. With more than enough wars under my belt, over the years I developed my personal rules of engagement.

- Avoid caustic statements that you will regret.

- Don't create a line in the sand or fixed position; flexibility is key.

- Keeping targets small results in fewer enemies.

- Avoid kill shots or gotchas.

- Compliment your counterpart... you're a smart person...

- Apologies for them... I am sorry you feel that way...

- Go silent and just listen and nod and try to understand.

- Speak with confidence and facts, not decibels.

- Stay away from conditions.

- Always keep the door open for new ideas.

- Strive for unity.

- Restrain from a counterpunch.

Create your own list of bomb diffusions. Try to understand what sets you off personally and what would calm you down for a positive outcome and apply it to a conflict.

So, what's the point? The point is war will happen and as General George Washington would say, "To be prepared for war is one of the most effective means of preserving peace." With any tension, there can be relief. Not many normal people enjoy constant conflict and beg for calm. I look at the concept of cause and effect. I encourage you to study the cause of tension and conflict, but more important the lasting effects they will have. The effect can crush a deal and ruin a relationship or with the right approach enhance a deal and strengthen a friendship. Look for a happy ending.

FINAL
APPROACH

Earlier in this book, I mentioned my ambition to be a private airplane pilot. If it wasn't for dealing with the takeoffs and landings, I think I would have made myself a mighty fine pilot, but the reality was that I never felt comfortable flying. I think a lot of people feel that way when they are involved in a dispute or negotiation. The plain fact (no pun intended) is that most people don't like to deal with conflict or confrontation, which is understandable. Because of this, they take the path of least resistance to avoid the pain and avoid conflict. My choice of ending my flying lessons was easy; I didn't feel comfortable doing it. I didn't need it and the consequence of a crash simply was not worth it for me. But for all of us, dealing with people, negotiations, and handling disputes on any level is an everyday part of life. So, we need to get good at it with a coherent plan and practice. To me, negotiations are like flying a plane. In both situations, if you make a mistake, you may crash. The difference is, that if you crash a negotiation, you may lose a deal. If you crash the plane, you may lose your life. Let's look at the similarities with flying: you prepare a flight plan, use a checklist (CIGARS), figure out your final destination, takeoff, maneuver to your destination, encounter turbulence, make a series of corrections, prepare for the descent to your destination, see it, work on the final approach, and land. Negotiating is the same. Start with what you want or what you want to achieve, create a plan, study your checklist (RAPPARS POINT), prepare for your opening remarks, engage in the dialogue, there may be some turbulence requiring some adjustments, prepare to close the deal, and, at the right moment, ask for an agreement or a yes.

The problem with a plan is that there is never one plan that fits them all. Dealing with people is like dealing with the weather, which we all know can be unpredictable. In dealing with so many personalities, it's not only the plan but also the approach. In this book, I have talked about a lot of techniques to get people to feel comfortable with dealing with you, but all that is for naught if you do not have the ability to ask for the deal, or better yet, the ability to close the deal. The reality is, at some point, you have to land the plane, or fly around in circles until you run out of gas. For some, closing the deal comes naturally. For others, it's a challenge. So why do people hesitate? Is it the fear of rejection? Lack of confidence or simply not in their comfort zone? Who knows, but it's emotional just like the fear of flying. If it's not coming naturally, you need to train and practice. Good communication is simply a result of well-thought questions and sincere and attentive listening. When I feel I have approached a time when the discussions we are having seem comfortable, creative, and conclusive, I call that the closing zone. That's the point when I need to ask the hard question to get a yes: Do we have an agreement? Music to my ears; however, what is the right question to ask? As a good lawyer would say, it depends on who you're dealing with. Below is a list of simple questions I have asked, looking for a yes.

- Do we have a deal?

- Would you like to move forward with this?

- Shall we write her up?

- Is this something you can live with?

- Is this good timing for you?

- I think this is a fair deal for both of us, do you agree?

- Can I assume we have a deal?

- Are you ready to come on board with us?

- Does this fit into your budget?

- Should we wrap this up?

- Have we covered everything?

- Are you comfortable with this?

- Shall I have our legal team prepare the paperwork?

- Does this fit all of your needs?

- I think we did a great job with this; do you agree?

Maybe these sound a little corny to you. But no problem, develop your own. Everyone has their own style and delivery system. The bottom line is that at some point you need to ask the closing question whether you like it or not. One of my favorite sales trainers said it's all about systems and dialogues, meaning having a standard system for approach and carefully personalized words for communication, and he was spot on.

So, what's the point? In a previous chapter, we talked about the concept of agreeing to agree. That is the place where both parties are on the same page as their desire to do a deal. This chapter's goal is to get you to go to the next step and actually agree on a deal. With RAPPARS POINT as your guideline, you will slowly and meticulously navigate your way to the closing zone, figure out what is the most appropriate closing question, and then give it a whirl. You have two options, don't ask, don't get, or ask and thou shall receive. Your choice.

FINAL
THOUGHTS...

As I progressed through writing this book, I questioned myself: Is this a book on negotiations, dispute resolution, or sales? I came to the conclusion that it's all of the above. However, the real focus is on how to effectively deal with people. The challenge and excitement of deal-making is that whatever you're trying to negotiate, resolve, or sell, you need to deal with people. What impedes that challenge is that each and every one of the folks you are going to deal with is different. More complicated is that these folk's moods will fluctuate daily. In the debate to find a mutual conclusion, whatever the topic, I have found that the first step is to simply do your best to get along with your counterpart. I know that may sound naive, but trying to agree should not be the same as a boxing match, as some would like it, but just a cordial exchange of ideas with a common desire for a good outcome. I believe that if you enter into a negotiation with infectious optimism, that will set the stage for your desired result. However, one of the questions you need to answer for yourself is, does your counterpart or the player you're dealing with really want to consummate a deal? Yes, that's a hard question to answer, but much needed to figure out. As inappropriate as it seems, people will come to the table, for whatever reasons, with no intention of doing a deal. Whether it's for show or saving face it happens. Even worse, they will come to the table with unreasonable terms and conditions with the attitude that they're going to throw all their crazy ideas at you, and if you should jump at them, great. If not, they will simply move on. They simply want to prey upon the weak and desperate and look for a one-sided deal. It's best to get this question out of the way as soon as possible if your gut is telling you there is a problem brewing. It's not unusual for someone to say to their counterpart, I sense that you are not willing to have a productive negotiation at this time, so I think it's best for us to shake hands and move on. That is the situation where one hopes for a decent, strong Plan B.

I believe that the wise negotiator or dispute resolution person should have the mindset that if there is a problem, we can figure it out and if there is an issue, we can work it out. In order to have that common give and take attitude, there needs to be a foundation of respect and the creation of a working relationship. To some, giving respect right from the get-go is a hard pill to swallow. It's like the chicken and the egg theory, which comes first? Some say that you have to earn and work for respect first, but my experience is that you give it right out of the gate and accept the risk of being taken advantage of. Why? Because I want to save a step in the relationship-building process and avoid any stressful mental gymnastics in developing trust. I simply want to be able to deal with the person first, before I attempt to deal with the problem or the product.

Early on in my career, I was involved with a lot of new construction condominium projects. I dealt with many builders and tradesmen and eventually joined our State Homebuilders Association and got involved with their sales and marketing council. Most of their focus was on how to properly market the developments and build traffic to their sales centers or model homes. In time, we got pretty good at our marketing campaigns to drive qualified prospects to our developments, but we still had a big problem, converting those prospects to buyers. We weren't the only ones with that problem, as it was a national concern. At some point, someone on the Sales and Marketing council decided to survey buyers that left projects without buying and ask them why they did not buy. To no surprise, answers included the price, location, floorplans, and features. The biggest surprise, however, was that for a high percentage of those responding, it was because they did not like the salesperson or their approach. Wow, we were spending a small fortune on marketing and doing a decent job of driving prospects to our developments, only to get axed by our own salespeople. At that time, I was the Vice President of marketing for a large construction company and my job performance depended on the success of my salespeople and the numbers were not in my favor. I immediately went to each of our developments and met personally with the salespeople and told them that for the next 30 days we were suspending all of our marketing efforts and instead focusing on all the people that had visited our model centers. We are going to personally invite them back for a private tour and offer them some kind of incentive for their trouble. We did have in place a system for obtaining their contact information, so it was just a matter of making phone calls... no emails, letters, or texts. The next step was to re-train our sales staff to focus on the prospect first, not our product. I think that the problem was that the sales force perceived that they only had a short period of time with the prospect, so they needed to hard sell, which raised the buyer's defense shields and created tension with no sale. I went on to explain that I wanted all of the sales staff to slow down with prospects, take the time and patience to focus on the buyer's personal situation, give respect,

FAILED TO NEGOTIATE THE DEAL

and build a relationship with them to better understand their needs. I asked them to create a relaxed environment where the buyers could be open and honest. I said it's all about them, not our product. You can't effectively deal with people if you don't take the time to understand them. My 30-day experiment worked: not only did I save marketing money, we converted a lot of prospects into buyers.

So, what's the point? Whether it's negotiations, disputes, or sales, it's all about dealing with people. Developing and maintaining great people skills is crucial to the process of crafting a deal or outcome that everyone is satisfied with. I figured out that deal creators are always subject to critiques, yet critics, typically are not deal creators, but deal busters. To achieve a healthy collaboration, someone needs to take charge as the deal creator, knowing that is simply a start. I want the deal to be a win for me, however, not at the expense of my counterpart. You need them to feel as though they have a win also, through mutual efforts to find common ground and expand the deal as best as possible. But it's an absolute must to have a great relationship and be in a no-judgment zone so you can get to that place. I have learned over time not to take the whole process too seriously and do my best to keep the relationship civil and friendly and not be afraid to change my approach if I feel we are going in the wrong direction. I prepare for and expect tension. I do my best to lower the temperature and yet keep my expectations high. It's been said that nice guys finish last, but I disagree. In negotiations, disputes, and sales I believe nice guys finish well, it's simply about being honest, sincere, and speaking from your heart.

I hope all of my ideas, thoughts, and stories resonate with you, for, in the end, I wish you all the luck in successfully negotiating the deal.

Points of Interest

PAUL HAMBLETT

....
....
....
....
....
....
....
....
....
....
....
....
....
....
....
....
....
....
....
....
....
....
....
....

FAILED TO NEGOTIATE THE DEAL

About the Author

Paul Hamblett has been in the real estate business in New England for over 40 years in many capacities including Brokerage, Property Management, Developer, and Builder. Paul was the Divisional Vice President of Sales and Marketing for a multi-billion construction company based in the UK. He was also the Owner/Broker of RE/MAX Coast to Coast, an award-winning real estate company based in Southern NH. Paul has personally negotiated thousands of real estate transactions, leases, and employment contracts.

Millie and me at the top of Cadillac Mountain, Acadia National Park.
Photo credit: Sue Haberstroh

At a very early age, Paul was consumed with negotiation skills and training after attending an Herb Cohen, author of the book "You Can Negotiate Anything," Seminar. He developed a strong, keen instinct in working with both sides of the negotiating table to achieve mutually desirable results. His ability to listen and understand the needs of his counterpart and create a relaxed atmosphere has resulted in expanding interests and options creating further value in deal-making. People first, then product or problem is his sequence for negotiation success.

Paul is an alumnus of Harvard Law School's Program on Negotiation and also completed Harvard Law School Negotiation Masters Class.

Paul resides in the small island town of New Castle, NH, where he continues to negotiate real estate deals, investment, and commercial leases.

My favorite negotiation and dealmaking books,
in no particular order.

Dealmaking
Guhan Subramanian

....

The Power of a Positive No
William Ury

....

Good for You, Great for Me
Lawrence Susskind

....

Getting to Yes
Roger Fisher and William Ury

....

Beyond Winning
Robert Mnookin

....

The Point of the Deal
Danny Ertel and Mark Gordon

....

3D Negotiation
David Lax and James Sebenius

....

You Can Negotiate Anything
Herb Cohen

....

Difficult Conversations
Sheila Heen, Douglas Stone, and Bruce Patton

....

Negotiating the Nonnegotiable
Daniel Shapiro

....

Built to Win
Lawrence Susskind and Hallam Movius

....

Beyond Reason
Roger Fisher and Daniel Shapiro

....

The Art of War
Sun Tzu

....

Thanks for the Feedback
Sheila Heen and Douglas Stone

....

Bringing Peace into the Room
Daniel Bowling and David Hoffman

....

Tip and The Gipper
Chris Matthews

....